MASONRY UNMASKED

MASONRY UNMASKED

AN INSIDER REVEALS
THE SECRETS OF THE LODGE

JOHN SALZA

Our Sunday Visitor Publishing Division
Our Sunday Visitor, Inc.
Huntington, Indiana 46750

TO JOHN SALZA, MY GRAMPS:

While you were here, you knew and lived the Truth.
Now you behold Him for all eternity.
Your prayers from heaven inspire and support me.
Thank you for your witness and love.

TABLE OF CONTENTS

PREFACE

There is much confusion among the faithful, both lay and religious, regarding the status of Catholic and Christian membership in Freemasonry. In the United States, the local Masonic lodge is often seen as nothing more than "a boys' club," where men perform trivial rituals, learn secret handshakes, and conduct fund-raising activities. The organization does not seem much different from the Lions Club or the Knights of Columbus. American lodges in recent years have not had a history of anti-Catholic agendas aimed at undermining the Church, as have their European and Latin American counterparts. Why, then, has the Catholic Church condemned Freemasonry? Why has every other Christian church that has seriously investigated the teachings of Freemasonry opposed membership in "the Lodge"?

This book provides answers to these questions by examining the religious and moral teachings of American Freemasonry in light of Christianity in general and the Catholic faith in particular. Notwithstanding the Church's declaration that Masonic principles are irreconcilable with Catholic doctrine, many still believe that the Church no longer opposes Freemasonry, and there are still Catholic and other Christian men who join the Lodge in good faith. Those who are aware of the Church's opposition often do not understand the religious and moral issues involved and, thus, are ineffective in helping those looking for answers. When I was a Mason and began having second thoughts about my membership in the Lodge, I struggled to find someone who could explain the Church's objections to Masonry. The need for such a resource prompted me to write this book.

While the basic teachings of Freemasonry are the same everywhere, this book focuses primarily on American Freemasonry. According to the organization's own most recent estimates, the United States has more Freemasons (about four million of the six million Masons worldwide) and Masonic organizations than any other country. Thus, American Masonry represents the majority of the world's Freemasonry, and provides a preeminent basis for our study. Further, having spent many hours studying, performing, and teaching Masonic ritual, I have firsthand knowledge of the doctrines and practices of American Masonic lodges.

I limit this examination to the first three degrees of American Freemasonry that are conferred in every Masonic lodge in the United States. I do not examine in detail the higher Masonic degrees (such as those conferred by the Scottish or York Rites) because most American Masons do not receive those degrees and knowledge of them is not crucial to comprehending Masonry's incompatibility with Christian faith. The focus, instead, is on the basics: what every American Mason learns in his lodge. This book also examines the conspiratorial nature of Freemasonry and how its efforts have contributed to the removal of Judeo-Christian principles from our public schools.

Many books have been written about Freemasonry, but none, to my knowledge, by a Catholic who left the Lodge. I approach this subject matter from a Catholic point of view, but the Church's reasons for condemning Masonry are consistent with those of other Christian traditions. My non-Catholic brothers and sisters in Christ should also find information in this book useful.

I have been encouraged to write this book by many people whose lives have been affected by Freemasonry. These people include family members whose husbands, fathers, and brothers are members of the Lodge; priests and pastors looking for understanding of the issues; and even Masons who are currently questioning their Masonic affiliation. While I do not wish to offend my former lodge brothers, this book will undoubtedly make some of them angry. I am certain that their reaction will be based, not on inaccuracies in my presentation, but on the fact that I promised — I was misled into promising — to keep these things secret. Yet any honest Mason should acknowledge that the biggest secret in Freemasonry is that there are no secrets. Most of the information presented in this book can be obtained from libraries, bookstores, and Grand Lodges throughout the country.

I am deeply grateful for the prayers and assistance of many people who were a part of my journey out of Freemasonry. I would especially like to thank Colin Donovan, S.T.L., for engaging me in debate when I was a Mason. Our exchanges prompted me to dig more deeply into my faith. Many thanks to former Mason Duane Washum for helping me through the difficulties of severing ties with the Lodge, and for assisting me with compiling and reviewing many of the Masonic authorities cited in this book. Thanks to Father Dan Sherman for the prayer sessions and discussions during my struggles with Masonry. Thanks to Gino Fazzari, Joe Calarco, Tom Glorioso, and Dan Maurina, fellow ex-Masons and brothers in Christ, for their support and input. Finally, I want to thank Father Paul Grizzelle-Reid, S.C.J., my dear friend, for encouraging me to bring this project to fruition.

JOHN SALZA
April 23, 2006
Divine Mercy Sunday

We wish it to be your rule first of all
to tear away the mask from Freemasonry,
and to let it be seen as it really is.

— POPE LEO XIII

Chapter

I

MY MASONIC CREDENTIALS

I was initiated as an Entered Apprentice Mason on June 24, 1996, at James M. Hays Lodge No. 331, in Wisconsin, on the feast of St. John the Baptist, my patron saint. I advanced to the degree of Fellowcraft on September 16, 1996, and became a Master Mason on October 14, 1996. On November 2, 1996, I was made a 32nd-degree Mason in the Scottish Rite. On December 7, 1996, I continued my Masonic journey by becoming a member of the Ancient Arabic Order of Nobles of the Mystic Shrine ("Shriners"). I also received a plural membership in Nathan Hale Lodge No. 350, where I became a lodge officer.

For the next three years, Freemasonry was one of the most important things in my life. I truly loved the organization and dedicated almost all of my available time to furthering its causes. My involvement took many forms but primarily focused on teaching Masonic ritual and conferring the three Masonic degrees. My Grand Lodge awarded me the Proficiency Card sooner — within a year of my initiation — than anyone in Wisconsin history. A Proficiency Card is a rare credential given to those Masons who can accurately perform from memory every facet of each of Freemasonry's three symbolic degrees. This involves memorizing several hundred pages of Masonic lectures, charges, and physical movements required to be made about the lodge ("rod and floor work"). This credential also authorizes the cardholder to give instruction on how to properly exemplify a Masonic degree.

I spent countless hours mastering Masonic ritual — memorizing, teaching, conferring degrees, and participating in various schools of instruction and degree competitions. I was also responsible for instituting many revisions of our jurisdiction's Masonic ritual. I served my lodge as Junior Deacon, Senior Deacon, and Junior Warden, and was to be elected Worshipful Master for the year 2000. I also participated in major roles in the Scottish Rite and the Shrine.

I really enjoyed the intellectual challenge of memorizing a complex lecture, perfecting my delivery, and presenting the degree to the candidate before my Masonic brothers. This exhilarating exercise, for which I gained a great deal of recognition, reminded me of the camaraderie I felt when I played organized sports. Admittedly, I had spiritual concerns during my own initiation into Masonry. The names for God, the prayers, the oaths, and the repeated references to eternal life were all vaguely troubling. But these concerns faded as I became increasingly fascinated with the rituals, the secrecy, the regalia, the controversy, the history, the unique bonds of brotherhood, and the rest of the Masonic pomp and circumstance. My ego became the driver, and as I gained in Masonic prowess, my spiritual concerns decreased. I had big plans for Masonry, and Masonry had big plans for me.

Occasionally, I would come across an anti-Masonic article or Web site, but I would quickly dismiss such attacks as religious fanaticism. I saw those people as intolerant, judgmental, and mean-spirited Bible thumpers with whom I had nothing in common. After all, some of the most admirable men of our society belonged to this secret fraternity. Therefore these anti-Masons were misinformed. I was enjoying fine friendships with my lodge brothers; how could something that felt so right be so wrong? At the time, I thought it couldn't be, and for three years I was one of Masonry's biggest apologists, bringing family and friends into the organization, and championing its cause as the greatest and most honorable fraternity in the world.

During my tenure, I frequently heard my lodge brothers comment on the Catholic Church's position on Masonry. While the Church had once opposed Catholic membership in Freemasonry, so I was told, it had reversed its position and now had no objections to the fraternity. I was also told that several popes had been Masons, as had many cardinals, bishops, priests, and monks. In order to be a papal Swiss Guard, I was informed that one had to be a Mason.

Though I certainly considered myself Catholic (I had twelve years of Catholic education), I never gave the tension between Freemasonry and the Church much thought. I was satisfied with what my lodge brothers told me and didn't feel compelled to investigate the matter any further. Rome seemed far away from my Masonic lodge, and I was sure that any objections the Vatican might have had in the past were based on misinformation.

Just to be certain, I called my parish priest and asked whether I could be a Mason, assuring him that I saw nothing in the lodge room that would be incompatible with my Catholic faith. Although he hadn't studied the matter, he too indicated that the Church had no objections to my membership in Masonry. Finally, I wasn't aware of any Catholic books that addressed the subject of Freemasonry. It seemed that all of the anti-Masonic books and Web sites were promoted by radical Christian fundamentalists.

My enthusiasm for Freemasonry continued to flourish. In addition to being an expert in Masonic ritual, I strove to become well versed in Masonic history and philosophy. I therefore researched topics of interest and prepared reports to present to the lodge as well as for my own enjoyment. During these research projects, I continued to come into contact with what I called anti-Masonic propaganda. While, deep down, I would relate to some of the issues these people raised, I quickly dismissed most of them as absurd. I was having the time of my life, and no one was going to tell me that being a Mason was contrary to the Christian faith.

Because I wanted to be a resource for the lodge on any Masonic topic, I decided to study the Christian arguments against Masonry. Then I would be prepared to answer such questions for my Christian lodge brothers as they came up. As an attorney, I knew I needed to have an open mind when studying the anti-Masonic position in order to cross-examine it effectively and, ultimately, destroy it. On a deeper level, though, I sensed that I was searching for something that would allow me to rationalize my own increasing involvement with the organization. Hence, the genesis of this book was really my effort to defend Freemasonry to myself.

To that end, I began to try to understand Scripture in light of my knowledge of Masonic ritual. I immediately identified passages that appeared to be incompatible with Masonry, such as our Lord's teachings about prayer, oaths, and eternal life. These were things I had learned throughout my childhood. But because my doctorate was in jurisprudence and not biblical theology, I had doubts about my scriptural exegesis. I knew and respected many other educated Christian Masons, however, and decided to seek their views.

In particular, I had developed a friendship with a very knowledgeable gentleman, an ordained Protestant clergyman who had been a Mason for over thirty years and held a master of divinity degree. Because he was well versed in both Christianity and Freemasonry, I was certain that he would be able to help me. I confided that I had concerns about Freemasonry's compatibility with Christianity. To assist, I provided him with extensive written analyses comparing certain scriptural passages with specific Masonic teachings. To my surprise, notwithstanding his many years of theological training, my brother was unable to defend Freemasonry. To him, Freemasonry was "just a fraternity," and that was all that mattered.

So I continued to raise questions with other respectable men of Masonry, including Past Masters, the Grand Lecturer, and even the Grand Master. Not one Mason was able to provide plausible answers. Most of them weren't even aware of the content of the Masonic rituals! Many even denied that the rituals taught religious ideas, even when I presented them chapter and verse. They told me I was taking it too far. I began to feel desperate to find someone who could provide the rationale I needed to remain in Masonry with a clear conscience.

Next I began to study the teachings of the Church. While my parish priest had told me it was acceptable to be a Mason, I was no longer satisfied. I started looking for a priest who had actually studied the question. Unable to find any such priest, I grew more desperate. At long last I became acquainted with Colin Donovan, a theologian who worked for the Eternal Word Television Network and who had knowledge of the subject of Freemasonry. We debated back and forth for over a month. Now I was really confused.

In my studies of the Church's teachings, I discovered that everything my Masonic brothers told me about the Church's position on Masonry appeared to be inaccurate. I found no evidence that any pope, cardinal, bishop, priest, or monk had ever been in Masonry. I learned that the claim concerning the Swiss Guards and their requirement to be Masons was untrue. Things began to unravel. I also discovered that the Congregation for the Doctrine of the Faith had issued a declaration prohibiting Catholic membership in Freemasonry and affirming what the Church had taught about Masonry for almost three hundred years.

Why, then, had my brothers told me that the Church now permitted membership, and why had my parish priest not known about the Church's position? Perhaps the Church's declarations were somehow not authoritative or binding. If I could prove that this rejection of Masonry was not official Church teaching, I rationalized that I was not bound to follow it. Given the apparent confusion on this question, my lawyer's mind was ready to find the loophole that would satisfy my conscience. This book sets forth my findings.

As soon as I made the decision to empty myself and seek the truth, God began to move me with his grace. This was no longer an academic exercise. The Lord touched my heart. I have chosen not to write about the personal aspects of my journey, preferring to let the Church and the Masonic rituals speak for themselves. But given my passion for Freemasonry, the countless hours I invested in the organization, and the goals I wanted yet to achieve within it, my experience has truly convinced me of the glory and mercy of God and his awesome power in changing the heart of a man who never expected that to happen.

Chapter

II

AN INTRODUCTION TO FREEMASONRY

A Brief History of Freemasonry

The true origins of Freemasonry are debated. Legend traces Freemasonry back to the builders of King Solomon's Temple, but most Masons do not believe there is any actual historical connection. Many Masonic historians claim Freemasonry originated with various ancient groups, such as the Dionysian artificers, the Pythagoreans, the Essenes, the Roman Collegia, the Commacine Masters, and the Druids. Other historians think Freemasonry rose out of the ancient pagan mystery religions. A tenable case can be made that Masonry's ties to the ancient mystery religions were preserved through the movements of Kabbalism, Gnosticism, the Knights Templar, the Rosicrucians, and the Illuminati. However, most Masonic historians of today trace the origins of Freemasonry to the stonemasons who built the great cathedrals of medieval Europe. Those men became known as "free masons" because, unlike the local guild masons, they were not indentured servants.

According to Masonic tradition, these "free masons" organized themselves into lodges. As time went by, outsiders — including philosophers, merchants, and bankers — were admitted to their group. These were called "accepted" masons. Gradually, the composition of the organization of "Free and Accepted Masons" changed from "operative" masons (those who built physical structures) to "speculative" masons (those who build the "spiritual temple," a Masonic metaphor for the soul). Today Freemasonry is completely speculative, although its operative heritage is referenced through ceremonial use of such tools as the square, level, plumb, compass, and trowel.

Modern Freemasonry was born in London on June 24, 1717, during the heart of the Enlightenment period. On that day, the Grand Lodge of England was founded, formally marking the transition from operative to speculative Freemasonry. This Grand Lodge, known as the "Modern Grand Lodge," developed the blueprint for today's Masonic rituals and ceremonies, including conferral of the three degrees: Entered Apprentice, Fellowcraft, and Master Mason. Certain Masonic dissidents, claiming that the rituals of the new Grand Lodge de-Christianized the Craft, set up the rival Ancient Grand Lodge. The two Grand Lodges coexisted as rivals from 1751 to 1813, when they merged to form the United Grand Lodge of Ancient Freemasons of England. By 1750, Freemasonry had already found its way to America, with chartered lodges in Boston and Philadelphia.

Today, all regular lodges throughout the world trace their origins to the Grand Lodge of England. A regular lodge is one that confers the three universally recognized Masonic degrees and has maintained the basic doctrines, rites, and modes of recognition established by the Mother Lodge of England. These regular lodges, with very few exceptions, also mandate universal recognition of one another. In Masonic parlance, *recognition* means that one Grand Lodge considers another Grand Lodge to be practicing valid Freemasonry. This also means that a Grand Lodge permits its own members to visit and participate in the Masonry of any recognized lodge. The most notable exception to universal recognition involves Prince Hall Grand Lodges, which are almost exclusively made up of black Masons. While Prince Hall Masonry subscribes to the three symbolic degrees, it does not enjoy universal recognition.

Evidence shows that historical Masonry before the formation of the Grand Lodge of England was Christian. For example, the Harleian MS. No. 1942 (about 1670) and the Antiquity MS. (1686), two of Masonry's oldest documents, both provide prayers invoking the Blessed Trinity: "In the name of the Great and Holy God, the wisdome of the Son and the goodnesse of the holy Ghost three Persons & one God be with us now and forever. Amen."[1] Operative Masons during the period were generally of the religion of the region in which they worked, primarily Catholic and Protestant Europe.

By the beginning of the eighteenth century, however, Enlightenment philosophy had begun to sweep through Europe. This period was marked by a movement to free men's minds from the "oppression" of dogma and ecclesiastical authority in favor of discerning truth through the rational study of nature. Man was to fulfill his spiritual vocation by using his intellect to determine the faith he would follow. While a vague belief in the power of a supreme deity was retained, the revealed truths of the fall of man, redemption, grace, and eternal salvation were generally rejected. Religion was reduced to a system of ethical behavior, creeds to a common denominator of "natural religion," and theology to a philosophy of history. In England, Enlightenment thinkers drew on the new spirit of naturalism, rationalism, and deism expressed by men such as Thomas Hobbes and John Locke.

The Masonic rituals developed by the Grand Lodge of England reflect the influence of Enlightenment philosophy. Freemasonry's degrees eliminated Christian prayer and any references to the Catholic religion. A Mason now had only to

---

[1] The Antiquity MS., *Little Masonic Library*, Vol. 1, 39.

believe in the deistic "Great (or Grand) Architect of the Universe" and an afterlife. These were held to be self-evident truths engraved on the hearts of all men. This sheds light on why many of the founders of the Republic who were deists were also Freemasons, such as George Washington and Benjamin Franklin.

The paradigm shift from revelation to reason can be seen in Dr. James Anderson's *The Constitution of the Free-Masons*, published in London in 1723, a most important Masonic book of this early period. In the section "Charges of a Free-Mason," the *Constitution* provides that

> though in ancient Times, Masons were charg'd in every Country to be of the Religion of that Country or Nation, whatever it was, yet 'tis now thought more expedient only to oblige them to that Religion in which all Men agree, leaving their particular Opinions to themselves.[2]

But the philosophy underlying this newly organized Freemasonry went beyond Enlightenment rationalism. The modern form of Freemasonry conceived in 1717 has evolved into a religion. While it still requires its members to keep their "particular opinions to themselves," Freemasonry has developed its own doctrines about the nature of God and eternal life. Freemasonry has also formalized these principles into a body of Masonic ritual and practice that is adhered to throughout the world. These are discussed in Chapter IV.

The Organization of Freemasonry

The basic organizational unit of modern Freemasonry is the Blue lodge, or Symbolic lodge. The chief officer of the Blue lodge, the

---

[2] Ibid., 14-15.

Worshipful Master, is elected for a one-year term. The other officers of the lodge are the Senior Warden, Junior Warden, Secretary, Treasurer (or Secretary-Treasurer), Chaplain, Senior Deacon, Junior Deacon, Senior Steward, Junior Steward, Tiler, and Lodge Counselor. Some lodges also have a Marshal, an Organist, or a Soloist. There are approximately fifteen thousand Blue lodges in the United States.

Each Blue lodge in a particular state comes under the authority of its Grand Lodge, which is headed by the Most Worshipful Grand Master. In North America, each state (and the District of Columbia) is governed by its own sovereign Grand Lodge. Hence, there are fifty-one Grand Lodges in the United States. In a Blue lodge, under the authority of its Grand Lodge, the candidate studies for and receives Masonry's three degrees.

While no degree is considered higher than that of Master Mason, a Master Mason in good standing is eligible to receive additional Masonic degrees and orders from two appendant bodies: the Scottish Rite and the York Rite. Appendant bodies are supplemental, or auxiliary, organizations a man may join after becoming a Master Mason. Because Blue Lodge Freemasonry is considered the foundation of Masonic philosophy, every appendant Masonic body bases its teachings and rituals on the first three symbolic degrees.

The Scottish Rite, also known as the "College of Freemasonry," confers the fourth through thirty-second degrees (as well as the honorary thirty-third degree). The Scottish Rite is divided into the Northern Jurisdiction, which governs fifteen states, and the Southern Jurisdiction, which governs the other thirty-five states, the District of Columbia, and the U.S. possessions. Each Scottish Rite organization in the Northern Jurisdiction is made up of four separate bodies: the Lodge of Perfection, the Council of Princes of Jerusalem, the Chapter of Rose Croix, and the

Consistory. The bodies of the Southern Jurisdiction are the same, except that the Council of Kadosh replaces the Chapter of Rose Croix. Each body is responsible for conferring certain of the various higher degrees of the order. The York Rite, also known as "Original" or "Ancient Craft" Masonry, confers a series of degrees conferred by the Royal Arch Chapter, the Council of Royal and Select Masters, and the Commandery of Knights Templar. The Scottish and York Rites, like all Masonic organizations, share the belief that there is no higher degree than that of a Master Mason.

In North America, a 32nd-degree, or York Rite, Mason in good standing is eligible to join the Ancient Arabic Order of Nobles of the Mystic Shrine (A.A.O.N.M.S.), also known as the "Shriners." You will notice that the letters of this abbreviation, when rearranged as is done in Shrine ritual, spell A. M.A.S.O.N. Shriners thus emphasize that the foundation of their order is Freemasonry. In fact, Masons call the Shrine the "playground of Freemasonry." The basic organizational unit of the Shrine is the Temple, or Mosque, in recognition of Allah, the honored deity of the Shrine. All Shriners swear an oath to Allah on the Koran, promising, under gruesome symbolic penalties, never to disclose the secrets of the order. The Shriners are most notable for their red fezzes, elaborate costumes, and circus parades. The Shrine is also known for its sponsorship of hospitals and other philanthropic activities.

In the United States, Shriners in good standing may join two other Masonic organizations: the Royal Order of Jesters and El Hajj. These groups, while organized primarily for social activities, have their own secret rituals and require members to swear oaths. There are also Masonic auxiliary groups, such as the Order of the Eastern Star (for women), DeMolay (for boys), and Job's Daughters (for girls). Though not officially Freemasons, these groups espouse Masonic principles. They believe in the Great Architect, the immortality of the soul, and the rule of secrecy. Other Masonic groups include the Tall Cedars of Lebanon, the Mystic Order of Veiled Prophets of the Enchanted Realm (the Grotto), the Knights of Pythias, the Knights of the Red Cross of Constantine, the Independent Order of Odd Fellows, the Acacia Fraternity, the White Shrine of Jerusalem, the Order of the Rainbow, the Daughters of the Nile, and the Order of Amaranth.

Who Speaks for Freemasonry?

There is no authority that speaks for worldwide Freemasonry. There is also no single governing body over American Grand Lodges. Each United States Grand Lodge is sovereign. Through its rituals, laws, and other practices, each Grand Lodge speaks authoritatively for Freemasonry in its particular state.

Although all Grand Lodges operate independently, their teachings are essentially the same. This is because Freemasonry is built upon certain ancient, unalterable principles called "Landmarks." Landmarks are the universal rules of the Craft, existing from time immemorial, and handed down by oral tradition. Without them, Freemasonry's identity would be destroyed.

There is no consensus among Masons as to every single Landmark, yet approximately half of the Grand Lodges in the United States have adopted Dr. Albert Mackey's list of twenty-five. Mackey (1807-1881) gave Freemasonry five major books, including *An Encyclopedia of Freemasonry*. Some Grand Lodges have not formally adopted Landmarks because the fundamental principles of Masonry are considered unalterable. In their view, it is not necessary to adopt them, since what can be adopted can be repealed.

Grand Lodges agree that the Landmarks of Masonry must include a belief in God as the Great Architect of the Universe, the immortality of the soul, and the resurrection of the body. Other

Landmarks require the use of symbolism and allegory to teach moral and religious truth, secrecy, covenant oaths, and the absence of physical and mental defects as a requirement for Masonic candidacy. The most common Masonic Landmarks are found in Appendix C.

Because receiving the degrees is what makes a man a Mason, Masonic rituals are the primary authority to be evaluated in light of the teachings of the Church. Grand Lodges generally publish some or all of their rituals in books with ciphered texts that are to be memorized by the officers performing the degree work. Basic cryptography is often sufficient to decipher many of the passages. Each Grand Lodge employs a Grand Lecturer to instruct the lodges in his state and to ensure that the ritual is being properly performed. Grand Lodges also include ritual work and explanatory materials in books called "monitors."

Although there is no exact uniformity of Masonic ritual, the differences from state to state are trivial. These would include trifling word variations, such as the phrase "having my heart plucked out" as opposed to "having my heart and vitals taken thence." The Grand Lodges of the United States all recognize the uniformity of American Masonic ritual. As the Grand Lodge of Massachusetts says, "members share the common bond of having passed through the same degree work, rites and rituals. Because of this, members can find brother Masons wherever they go."[3] Whatever lodge a Mason visits, "the teachings and the basics will be the same."[4] Mackey affirms that "[t]he doctrine of Freemasonry is everywhere the same. It is the Body which is unchangeable — remaining always and everywhere the same."[5] Masonry's requirement of hav-

---

[3] Grand Lodge AF&AM, Massachusetts, "What It Means to Be a Mason," http://www.glmasons-Mass.org.

[4] Grand Lodge of North Carolina, http://www.grandlodge-nc.org.

[5] *Mackey's Revised Encyclopedia of Freemasonry*, Vol. 2, 859.

ing candidates pass oral examinations in open lodge regarding the esoteric teachings and practices of the Craft also perpetuates the uniformity of its rituals (Masonic Bible, p. 62). Kent Henderson, who has compiled a guide book for the traveling Freemason, says:

> The content of the Craft degrees as worked around the world is fairly similar, regardless of which ritual may be used. Every jurisdiction practises the three degrees of Entered Apprentice, Fellow Craft, and Master Mason. Every regular jurisdiction adheres to the Ancient Landmarks of the Order. Similarly, the legend of the Third Degree, the modes of recognition, and the general teachings of the Order are all constants.[6]

This book examines American Masonic ritual exclusively. Every Grand Lodge in the United States recognizes the rituals described herein as valid and universal Freemasonry. Rituals cited in this book are also recognized as regular Masonry by the prominent Grand Lodges of England, Ireland, and Scotland, among others.

Masonry's objective in recognizing or not recognizing other Grand Lodges throughout the world is to preserve the universality of its rituals and doctrines. For example, on September 14, 1877, the Grand Orient of France, that country's oldest Masonic organization, removed the requirement to believe in deity and the immortality of the soul. Consequently, most regular Grand Lodges throughout the world no longer recognized it as valid and regular Freemasonry, though the Grand Orient had previously enjoyed universal recognition since 1724.

---

[6] *Masonic World Guide — A Guide to Grand Lodges of the World for the Travelling Freemason*, 34.

I have stressed this point about uniformity in ritual because of the main tack used by Masonic apologists to defend Freemasonry against Christian opposition. When a Christian attempts to cite Masonic ritual to demonstrate an incompatibility between the Lodge and the Christian faith, the Mason is apt to exclaim, "No one speaks for Freemasonry" (which begs the question why he thinks he does). While it is true that no one organization formally speaks for American Freemasonry, each Grand Lodge, as has been said, speaks for Freemasonry in its particular state. Henry Wilson Coil confirms that "Grand Lodges are the highest Masonic authorities in both law and doctrine."[7] When this reality is presented to the Mason, his only options are to address the ritual in question or to remain silent. If he is presented with ritual from his own jurisdiction, he usually remains silent because he is sworn to secrecy. If he is presented with ritual from another state, he invariably feigns ignorance.

Ironically, if a Mason decides to challenge the validity of another state's ritual, his conduct is considered un-Masonic, since he has no authority to make such a challenge (only his Grand Lodge does). If his Grand Lodge recognizes the other state's ritual as valid — as is always the case for lodges in the United States — then the Mason is bound by his oath to concede that the jurisdiction is practicing valid Freemasonry. This is because every Mason swears to "maintain and support the edicts of his Grand Lodge." Every Mason also swears that he will not sit in a "clandestine lodge" or talk about the secrets of Masonry with a "clandestine Mason." The Mason can only fulfill this promise by respecting the edicts of recognition issued by his Grand Lodge. Therefore, an American Mason cannot criticize another state's Masonic ritual without also criticizing his own Grand Lodge and

---

[7] *Coil's Masonic Encyclopedia,* 569.

violating his Masonic obligation. Many Masons boast about Freemasonry's universality in its teaching and practice — until a Christian challenges its rituals on the basis of this universality.

Another significant authority used primarily in the United States to supplement the teachings of Masonic ritual is the Masonic Bible, which is made up of the Old and New Testaments (King James Version) and an extensive section on the dogmas and ritualistic practices of the Craft. It is easily identified by the prominent Masonic symbol on the cover and/or spine of the book.

In the United States, the Masonic Bible is traditionally presented in a formal ceremony to all newly made Master Masons. Typically, this is the Bible on which the candidate swears his third-degree oath. The Masonic Bible primarily used by Grand Lodges in the United States is the Heirloom Masonic Bible (Master Reference Edition, DeVore & Sons, Inc., 1988), which is sold by distributors of Masonic supplies. I use this Bible in evaluating the teachings of Freemasonry in light of the Catholic faith in particular and Christianity in general.

I also use explanations of Masonic ritual provided by the Masonic Service Association of North America, or the MSA. Formed in 1919, the MSA's primary function is to educate Masons and the public concerning Freemasonry by providing free publications, including the *Short Talk Bulletin* series, on various Masonic topics. These publications, which serve Freemasonry throughout North America, are valuable resources for anyone who wants to learn the teachings of the Craft.

Finally, I quote from authors recognized and recommended by Freemasonry. In addition to Dr. Mackey, the most prominent Masonic authors are Albert Pike and Henry Wilson Coil. Pike (1809-1891) is considered the Father of Scottish Rite Freemasonry, in which he served as Sovereign Grand Commander of the Southern Jurisdiction from 1859 until his death. Pike is remembered for his Masonic opus *Morals and Dogma of the Ancient and Accepted Scottish Rite of Freemasonry.*[8] Henry Wilson Coil (1885-1974) edited the considerable work *Coil's Masonic Encyclopedia.* These are also the authorities the Catholic Church uses in its studies on Freemasonry.[9]

Therefore, in fairness to Freemasonry, I evaluate its compatibility with Christianity by relying in my analysis on Masonry's own recognized rituals, practices, and authors. I allow Freemasonry to speak for itself.

---

[8] The Grand Lodge of Arkansas, in whose state Pike spent most of his life, gives the Albert Pike award for the best Masonic Web sites for content, images, graphics, and fonts.

[9] See, for example, William J. Whalen, "The Pastoral Problem of Masonic Membership," *Origins*, 15/6 (June 27, 1985), 84-92.

Chapter

III

THE IDEOLOGY OF FREEMASONRY

Introduction to the Problem of Indifferentism

Freemasonry's stated aim is to help make good men better by teaching them universal truths. The Masonic Service Association defines Freemasonry as "an organization of men believing in the Fatherhood of God and the Brotherhood of Man, using the builder's tools as symbols to teach basic moral truths, thereby impressing upon the minds of its members the cardinal virtues of Brotherly Love, Relief, and Truth."[1]

In its effort to make good men better, Masonry announces that its mission is "to promote a way of life that binds like-minded men in a worldwide brotherhood that transcends all religious, ethnic, cultural, social and educational differences."[2] The Masonic Bible (p. 62) says, "The real object of Freemasonry, in a philosophical and religious sense, is the search for Truth." Albert Mackey describes Masonry as "a science which is engaged in the search after Divine Truth, and which employs symbolism as its method of instruction."[3]

---

[1] *The Short Talk Bulletin*, "What Does Freemasonry Offer the World?" Vol. 43, No. 8 (1965).

[2] Grand Lodge of Arizona Free and Accepted Masons, "The Mission of Freemasonry," http://www.azmasons.org.

[3] *Mackey's Revised Encyclopedia of Freemasonry*, Vol. 1, 269.

The Church recognizes that the struggle to find the truth is part of the very essence of being a human being.[4] The *Catechism of the Catholic Church* informs us that all men are bound to seek the truth, especially religious truth, and to embrace it when they come to know it (cf. CCC 2104). Further, the Church actively promotes unity among the human family in spite of religious, ethnic, or cultural differences. But unlike the Church, which declares that the fullness of God's truth is found in the Person of Jesus Christ, the Lodge never defines for its members the religious "truth" it seeks. "Masonry," says Albert Pike, "must needs leave it to each of its initiates to look for the foundation of his faith and hope to the written scriptures of his own religion. For itself it finds those truths definite enough, which are written by the finger of God upon the heart of man and on the pages of the book of nature."[5]

Notwithstanding its relativism concerning religious truth (which is reason enough for the Church's condemnation), Masonry claims that the practice of its principles will advance a Mason's spirituality and help him get to heaven: "By the practice of Freemasonry," says the Masonic Bible (p. 26), "its members may advance their spirituality, and mount by the theological ladder from the Lodge on earth to the Lodge in heaven." Albert Mackey also says that its "rounds . . . present us with the means of advancing from earth to heaven, from death to life — from the mortal to immortality."[6] Henry Wilson Coil, Masonry's other prominent encyclopedist, adds that many Freemasons may have "no other guarantee of a safe landing than their belief in the religion of Freemasonry."[7]

---

[4] Cf. Pope John Paul II, encyclical, *Fides et Ratio* (September 14, 1998), No. 2.

[5] *Morals and Dogma of the Ancient and Accepted Scottish Rite of Freemasonry*, 226 (hereafter cited as *Morals and Dogma*).

[6] *Mackey's Revised Encyclopedia of Freemasonry*, Vol. 1, 499.

[7] *Coil's Masonic Encyclopedia*, 512.

Freemasonry, therefore, goes beyond promoting the common good; it moves into the realm of religion and soteriology (that part of theology dealing with salvation). The Lodge claims that its principles will advance its members to "the heavenly lodge above," but it requires no belief in Jesus Christ or his Church. The Mason has to possess only the minimum belief in a supreme being and eternal life after death. Faithful to its Enlightenment roots, the Lodge is indifferent to the revealed truths of the fall, original sin, the necessity of redemption, and the Incarnation of the Son of God, who declared, "I am the way, and the truth, and the life; no one comes to the Father, but by me" (Jn 14:6).

Freemasonry's view that all religions are competitive attempts to express the truth about God and equally effective in advancing one's spiritual life is known as *indifferentism*. Advocates of indifferentism maintain that God looks only at the sincerity of the person's intentions, not to his or her particular doctrinal beliefs. Indifferentism is premised on the notion that, beyond the fact of God's existence, we can know virtually nothing about God. This is because God, being infinite, is incomprehensible to our finite minds. Masonry reasons that there is no need to argue over any particular conception of him; God will be pleased with whatever form of worship we sincerely offer him.

The Masonic Service Association comments on the difficulty of expressing truths about God: "[A]ll that Masonry asks is that we confess our faith in a Supreme Being. It does not require that we analyze or define in detail our thought of God. . . . No man can put such things into words, much less into a hard and fast dogma."[8] Insisting that a true Mason's religion must be "universal," Manly P. Hall describes him as one who "worships at every shrine, bows before every altar, whether in temple, mosque or cathedral,

---

[8] *The Short Talk Bulletin*, "The Letter *G*," Vol. 5, No. 7, (1927).

realizing . . . the oneness of all spiritual truth."[9] To the true Mason, "Christ, Buddha, or Mohammed, the name means little."[10]

The Lodge considers any specific doctrines concerning God, beyond what can be known by nature and reason, to be "sectarian" innovations. As Joseph Fort Newton explains, "Masonry seeks to free men from a limited conception of religion, and thus to remove one of the chief causes of sectarianism."[11] *Sectarianism* is a pejorative term indicating that a religion so described is too limited in its scope. As Albert Mackey tells us, "[T]he religion of freemasonry is not sectarian. It admits men of every creed within its hospitable bosom, rejecting none and approving none for his particular faith. It is not Judaism . . . it is not Christianity." Albert Mackey calls the religious doctrines of Freemasonry "very simple and self-evident." They are not darkened, he says, by "perplexities of sectarian theology." Rather, they are "acceptable by all minds, for they ask only for a belief in God and in the immortality of the soul."[12]

Spared of the complexities of sectarianism, all men can unite and offer worship around the altar of Freemasonry: "Around it, all men, whether they have received their teachings from Confucius, Zoroaster, Moses, Mohammed or the founder of the Christian religion — just so long as they believe in the universality of the fatherhood of God and universality of the brotherhood of man — meet upon a common level." And as a result, each one is "better prepared for the solemn duties of life by the associations in this universal brotherhood."[13]

While Freemasonry may be said to demonstrate good intentions by promoting the unity of the human family and the spiri-

[9] *The Lost Keys of Freemasonry; or, The Secret of Hiram Abiff*, 65.
[10] Ibid.
[11] *The Builders: A Story and Study of Freemasonry*, 243.
[12] *An Encyclopedia of Freemasonry*, 731.
[13] Louisiana Monitor (1980), 133.

tual welfare of its members, God cannot be pleased with the Lodge's treatment of his revelation as superfluous and sectarian. This is because God is both eternal love and eternal truth. Out of his everlasting love for humanity, God willed both to reveal himself to man and to give him the grace of being able to welcome his revelation in faith (cf. CCC 35). Faith in God is a "*free assent to the whole truth that God has revealed*" (CCC 150; emphasis in original). God has thus engraved on our hearts the yearning for absolute truth and a thirst to attain full knowledge of it.[14]

Indifference to this truth is inconsistent with this yearning, and a grave injustice against God. God calls us into the fullness of his truth and love. "You shall love the LORD your God with all your heart, and with all your soul, and with all your might" (Deut 6:5). Because God's revelation in Jesus Christ is the ultimate expression of his love, to be indifferent to God's revelation is to be indifferent to God's love. For the Lodge, ironically, this means being indifferent to God himself, for "God is love" (1 Jn 4:8, 16).

The errors of indifferentism are exposed on an even more fundamental level if one accepts the reality that God, as omniscient Creator, is the source of all truth. Even if all religions represented in the Lodge were to contain some elements of this truth, it is erroneous for the Lodge to suggest that God, who is Truth, is indifferent to what a man believes. If that were the case, God's decision to reveal himself would mean little (unless we were to accuse God of doing meaningless things), and both truth and falsehood would be consonant with his nature. This denies who God is, "for God is not a God of confusion but of peace" (1 Cor 14:33).

Therefore, the Church has condemned indifferentism as a heresy on the grounds that it is contrary, not just to revelation, but

---

[14] Cf. Pope John Paul II, encyclical, *Veritatis Splendor* (May 25, 1995), No. 1.

to reason as well. Pope Pius VIII declared that "this deadly idea concerning the lack of difference among religions is refuted even by the light of natural reason. We are assured of this because the various religions do not often agree among themselves. If one is true, the other must be false; there can be no society of darkness with light."[15] This follows St. Paul's words: "For what partnership have righteous and iniquity? Or what fellowship has light with darkness? What accord has Christ with Belial? . . . Therefore come out from them, and be separate from them, says the Lord" (2 Cor 6:14-15, 17).

Blessed Pius IX describes as "perverse" the theory that it makes no difference to which religion one belongs:[16] "Nothing more insane than such a doctrine, nothing more impious or more opposed to reason itself could be devised. For although faith is above reason, no real disagreement or opposition can ever be found between them . . . because both of them come from the same greatest source of unchanging and eternal truth, God."[17]

In his encyclical on Freemasonry, Pope Leo XIII declared that the Masonic sects teach a great error — that religions are all alike: "This manner of reasoning is calculated to bring about the ruin of all forms of religion, and especially of the Catholic religion, which, as it is the only one that is true, cannot, without great injustice, be regarded as merely equal to other religions."[18]

While condemning the errors of indifferentism, the Church recognizes that our natural faculties enable us to know the existence of a personal God (cf. CCC 35). The First Vatican Council affirmed that God "can be known with certainty from the created world by the natural light of human reason."[19] On that most basic point, the

---

[15] Encyclical, *Traditi Humilitati* (May 24, 1829), No. 4.
[16] Encyclical, *Qui Pluribus* (November 9, 1846), No. 15.
[17] Ibid., No. 6.
[18] *Humanum Genus* (April 20, 1884), No. 16.
[19] *Dei Filius* (April 24, 1870).

Church and the Lodge agree. However, in the historical conditions in which he finds himself, man experiences difficulties in coming to know God by the light of reason alone. The human intellect is hampered in the attainment of such truths, "not only by the impact of the senses and the imagination, but also by disordered appetites which are the consequences of original sin. So it happens that men in such matters easily persuade themselves that what they would not like to be true is false or at least doubtful."[20] Revelation is necessary, the Church teaches, even "about those religious and moral truths which of themselves are not beyond the grasp of human reason, so that . . . they can be known by all men with ease, with firm certainty and with no admixture of error" (CCC 38).

Therefore, the Church condemns the idea that it is impossible or not expedient to be taught by means of God's divine revelation.[21] The Church notes that religious relativism is rooted in the conviction of the elusiveness and inexpressibility of truth.[22] This position holds that "truth about God cannot be grasped and manifested in its globality and completeness by any historical religion, neither by Christianity nor by Jesus Christ."[23] It is true that the mystery of God's revelation transcends our limited human understanding. But Masonry's conviction that God's truth is elusive, inexpressible, and ultimately unattainable is at odds with God's revelation in his only-begotten Son.

The Church teaches us that "the words, deeds and entire historical event of Jesus possess in themselves the definitiveness and completeness of the Revelation of God's salvific ways, even if the depth of the divine mystery in itself remains transcendent and

---

[20] Pope Pius XII, encyclical, *Humani Generis* (August 12, 1950), No. 2; cf. CCC 37.

[21] First Vatican Council, Session 3, Canon 2, *On Revelation* (April 24, 1870).

[22] CDF (Congregation for the Doctrine of the Faith), *Dominus Iesus* (August 6, 2000), No. 4.

[23] Ibid., No. 6

inexhaustible."[24] "The truth about God is also not abolished or reduced because it is spoken in human language; rather, it is unique, full, and complete, because he who speaks and acts is the Incarnate Son of God."[25] In fact, our faith is more certain than all human knowledge because it is founded on the very Word of God, who cannot lie (cf. CCC 157). Therefore, the Church, unlike the Lodge, teaches that we can know the truth about God definitively and completely, even if we cannot know it exhaustively.

Masonry's emphasis on God's incomprehensible transcendence is also a form of agnosticism, which assumes a number of forms. "In certain cases the agnostic refrains from denying God; instead he postulates the existence of a transcendent being which is incapable of revealing itself, and about which nothing can be said" (CCC 2127). When agnosticism is expressed as indifferentism, as it is in the Lodge, it can indicate a flight from the ultimate question of existence, and a sluggish moral conscience. "Agnosticism is all too often equivalent to practical atheism" (CCC 2128). Pope Pius XI taught that those who hold all religions to be good and praiseworthy, not only err, but in distorting the idea of true religion, they reject it and, little by little, turn to naturalism and atheism.[26]

The Church's appraisal of the religious teachings of the Lodge should not be viewed as a criticism of the right to religious freedom. The Church, like the Lodge, holds that the human person has a civil right to religious freedom, declaring that "all men are to be immune from coercion on the part of individuals or of social groups and of any human power, in such wise that no one is to be forced to act in a manner contrary to his own beliefs."[27] This civil right to freedom has "its foundation in the dignity of the person"

---

[24] Ibid.
[25] Ibid.
[26] Cf. encyclical, *Mortalium Animos* (January 6, 1928), No. 2.
[27] Second Vatican Council, *Dignitatis Humane* (December 7, 1965), No. 2.

and "its roots in divine revelation, and for this reason Christians are bound to respect it all the more conscientiously."[28]

But one cannot detach human freedom from its essential and constitutive relationship to truth. Jesus said that "you will know the truth, and the truth will make you free" (Jn 8:32). Without the objective reality of truth, there is no objective right to freedom. Because freedom is grounded in truth, the Church teaches that these God-given freedoms are not a license to adhere to error (cf. CCC 2108). While recognizing the *civil* right to religious freedom, man does not have a *moral* right to worship outside the parameters that God has revealed. As a result, religious freedom can never be used to defend the relativism of Freemasonry.

The Church does not deny that goodness and truth can be found in other religions. The Second Vatican Council says this: "The Catholic Church rejects nothing of what is true and holy in these religions. She has a high regard for the manner of life and conduct, the precepts and teachings, which, although differing in many ways from her own teaching, nonetheless often reflect a ray of that truth which enlightens all men."[29] Pope Paul VI, in his apostolic exhortation "On Evangelization in the Modern World," says that "the Church respects and esteems these non-Christian religions because they are the living expression of the soul of vast groups of people."[30]

But followers of other religions are, objectively speaking, in a gravely deficient situation in comparison with those who, in the Church, have the ordinary means of salvation.[31] This is why any goodness and truth that can be found in other religions must be used as "a preparation for the Gospel" (CCC 843). Immediately

---

[28] Ibid., No. 9.
[29] *Nostra Aetate* (October 28, 1965), No. 2.
[30] *Evangeli Nuntiandi*, (December 8, 1975), No. 53.
[31] Cf. Pope Pius XII, encyclical, *Mystici Corporis*, (June 29, 1943).

after the Second Vatican Council recognized the possibility of a "ray of truth" in other religions, it stated that the Church "ever must proclaim Christ 'the way, the truth, and the life' (Jn 14:6), in whom men may find the fullness of religious life, in whom God has reconciled all things to Himself."[32]

Because God wills the salvation of everyone through the knowledge of his truth, and the totality of this truth has been entrusted to the Church (cf. 1 Tim 3:15), the Church must labor against the errors of indifferentism. Christians cannot leave non-Christians in a state of partial-faith and half-truth. In this way, we fulfill the Lord's missionary mandate (cf. Mt 28:19-20; Mk 16:15) by proclaiming the whole truth of Jesus Christ and revealing the errors of Freemasonry.

The Second Vatican Council goes on to say:

> The disciple is bound by a grave obligation toward Christ, his Master, ever more fully to understand the truth received from Him, faithfully to proclaim it, and vigorously to defend it, never — be it understood — having recourse to means that are incompatible with the spirit of the Gospel.[33]

Pope Paul VI tells us that

> the presentation of the Gospel message is not an optional contribution for the Church. It is the duty incumbent on her by the command of the Lord Jesus, so that people can believe and be saved. This message is indeed necessary. It is unique. It cannot be replaced. It does not permit either indifference, syncretism or accommodation. It is a question of people's salvation.[34]

---

[32] *Nostra Aetate* (October 28, 1965), No. 2.
[33] *Dignitatis Humane*, No. 14.
[34] *Evangeli Nuntiandi*, No. 5.

Pope John Paul II also says that the respect we have for individuals "rules out, in a radical way, that mentality of indifferentism characterized by a religious relativism which leads to the belief that one religion is as good as another."[35]

Indifference Toward God and Jesus Christ

Freemasonry begins to exhibit its indifference toward Christ from the moment a candidate first enters the lodge room. When a candidate receives the Entered Apprentice degree, he is conducted into the lodge room, asked to kneel and make a profession of faith. The Worshipful Master places his left hand on the candidate's head and asks, "In whom do you put your trust?" If the candidate professes a belief in any "Supreme Being," the Worshipful Master says, "Your trust being in God, your faith is well-founded. Arise, follow your conductor, and fear no danger."

No matter what faith a candidate professes (assuming he is not an atheist), the Worshipful Master assures the candidate that his trust is in God because "Freemasonry reverences all titles by which God is known" (Masonic Bible, p. 44). Thus, one Mason's belief in a pantheistic god, for example, could flatly reject or contradict another Mason's monotheism, but Freemasonry declares to *both* that their faith is well-founded. Such a position is contrary to reason. If two Masons have incompatible beliefs about God and one of them is true, the other must necessarily be false. It cannot be "well-founded." It is also possible that both beliefs are false. To hold them both true, as the Lodge does, is to deny objective truth altogether. While Freemasonry claims to worship God "in spirit and in truth" (Masonic Bible, p. 55), the Lodge's teaching on truth contradicts the very definition of truth, which is exclusionary by its nature.

---

[35] Encyclical, *Redemptoris Missio* (December 7, 1990), No. 36.

As Pope John Paul II has stated, "A legitimate plurality of positions has yielded to an undifferentiated pluralism, based upon the assumption that all positions are equally valid, which is one of today's most widespread symptoms of the lack of confidence in truth."[36] The Masonic Service Association, on the other hand, has said, "One of the greatest truths man has learned, in all his centuries of study, is that there is no absolute to be known; all truths, including the mathematical, are relative."[37] Paradoxically, this relativistic notion of truth renders Masonry's self-professed object, truth, unattainable.

Of course, equating Christ with other gods also presumes that the revealed truths of Christianity have been superseded or are, at best, parallel with other traditions. But a confession of faith in Vishnu is not the same as a confession of faith in the Eternal Word made flesh. For the one, the search for God continues. For the other, the search is completed with the revelation of God's salvific mystery in the Lord Jesus Christ, "for in him the whole fullness of deity dwells bodily" (Col 2:9).

Masonry's idea of the equality of religions is based on the supposed equality of their founders. Jesus is thus viewed by the Lodge as no more than a "particular, finite, historical figure, who reveals the divine not in an exclusive way, but in a way complementary with other revelatory and salvific figures."[38] Pike states that Freemasonry reverently regards all the great reformers: "It sees in Moses, the Lawgiver of the Jews, in Confucius and Zoroaster, in Jesus of Nazareth, and in the Arabian Iconoclast, Great Teachers of Morality, and Eminent Reformers, if no more."[39]

Lynn Perkins offers us Freemasonry's view of Jesus Christ:

---

[36] Encyclical, *Fides et Ratio*, No. 5.
[37] *The Short Talk Bulletin*, "Masonic Geometry," Vol. 12, No. 5 (1934).
[38] CDF, *Dominus Iesus*, No. 9.
[39] *Morals and Dogma*, 525.

Though Avatars have come to all people at different times with the same essential message, nevertheless the Christian Avatar is still not acceptable to some peoples. . . . Jesus of Nazareth was sent to be a light to the world to some branches of the human race, but other branches have had, and do now have, their Buddha, their Krishna, their Zoroaster, their Confucius, their Mohammed.[40]

The Church is clear that placing Jesus of Nazareth on a par with other religious and moral reformers is in profound conflict with the Christian faith. Putting Jesus in the same category as other religious teachers, or "avatars," is not an option for us. Jesus told us that he is God: "Truly, truly, I say to you, before Abraham was, I am" (Jn 8:58); "I and the Father are one," (Jn 10:30). The Church affirms this: "The doctrine of the faith must be *firmly believed* which proclaims that Jesus of Nazareth . . . is the Son and Word of the Father."[41] If Jesus is God, his divine status is not shared with Mohammed, Buddha, or Confucius. If Jesus is not God, he is a blasphemer and a madman. There is no middle ground.

Masonry's notion of Christ as truth for only some people at a particular time is also at odds with the universal nature of truth. Pope John Paul II writes in his encyclical *Faith and Reason* (No. 27) that "every truth — if it is really truth — presents itself as universal, even if it is not the whole truth. If something is true, then it must be true for all people and at all times." Pike disagrees:

Catholicism was a vital truth in its earliest ages, but it became obsolete, and Protestantism arose, flourished and deteriorated. The doctrines of Zoroaster were the best which the ancient

---

40 *The Meaning of Masonry*, 54-55.
41 CDF, *Dominus Iesus*, No. 10 (emphasis in original).

Persians were fitted to receive; those of Confucius were fitted for the Chinese; those of Mohammed for the idolatrous Arabs of his age. Each was Truth for the time.[42]

While Freemasonry promotes the generic worship of the subjective God, the Christian Mason disclaims any responsibility in bearing witness to the objective truth of Jesus Christ. His attitude effectively embraces the errors of relativism and demonstrates a lack of charity to the lodge brothers he is oath-bound to serve.

In the face of the religious pluralism, indifferentism, and relativism of our current age, the Church, in the Jubilee Year 2000, reaffirmed the significance of Jesus for mankind: "Jesus Christ has a significance and a value for the human race and its history, which are unique and singular, proper to him alone, exclusive, universal, and absolute. Jesus is, in fact, the Word of God made man for the salvation of all."[43]

Indifference Toward the Holy Bible

Freemasonry also manifests its indifference toward divine revelation as found in Sacred Scripture. An altar is at the center of every Masonic lodge room. On it rests the Masonic Square, the Compasses, and what is called the Volume of the Sacred Law. In most Masonic lodges in the United States, this volume is the Holy Bible. Because Freemasonry views other religious writings as equally legitimate expressions of God's will, it offers them an equal place on the altar with the Bible. Whether it's the Book of Mormon, the Koran, the Vedas, the Zend Avesta, the Sohar, the Kabbalah, the Bhagavad Gita, the Upanishads, or any other religious writing, all are given center stage in the Masonic lodge room.

---

[42] *Morals and Dogma*, 38.
[43] CDF, *Dominus Iesus*, No. 15. See also Pope John Paul II, *Redemptoris Missio*, No. 6.

Coil's Masonic Encyclopedia says that "the Bible is only a *symbol* of Divine Will, Law or Revelation" (emphasis added). Coil says that Masonry does not believe the Bible's contents are "Divine Law, inspired, or revealed," and adds that "no responsible authority has held that a Freemason must believe the Bible or any part of it" (p. 520). Mackey also says that "the Bible is used among Masons as a symbol of the will of God, however it may be expressed. And, therefore, whatever to any people expresses that will may be used as a substitute for the Bible in a Masonic Lodge."[44]

The Christian Mason may wish to take comfort in the fact that his lodge displays the Bible at each meeting on the altar. Yet his view of Scripture can hardly be reconciled with that of the Lodge. Pike clarifies for the Mason why the Bible is only "part of the furniture" of the lodge: "The obligation [oath] of the candidate is always to be taken on the sacred book or books of his religion, that he may deem it more solemn and binding. . . . We have no other concern with your religious creed."[45]

In Freemasonry, the sacred texts are not authoritative, and no Mason, even if Christian, is required by the Lodge to believe in their divine inspiration. "In fact," writes George Wingate Chase, "Blue Lodge Masonry has nothing whatsoever to do with the Bible; it is not founded on the Bible. If it was, it would not be Masonry; it would be something else."[46] Oliver D. Street, a renowned Masonic scholar, offers a concise summary of Freemasonry's view of the Bible in words to this effect: The Bible is only a symbol; a Mason is not required to believe in its teachings; some other book may be substituted for it.[47]

---

[44] *An Encyclopedia of Freemasonry*, 114.
[45] *Morals and Dogma*, 11.
[46] *Digest of Masonic Law*, 206.
[47] Cf. "Freemasonry in Foreign Lands," in *Little Masonic Library*, Vol. 1, 129-30.

Freemasonry's view of the Holy Bible as a replaceable symbol of God's will rather than his divine revelation is incompatible with the Catholic faith in particular and Christianity in general. The Church teaches that "*God is the author of Sacred Scripture. The divinely revealed realities, which are contained and presented in the text of Sacred Scripture, have been written down under the inspiration of the Holy Spirit*" (CCC 105; emphasis in original; cf. 2 Tim 3:16). In fact, the Church dogmatically teaches that the words of Scripture were dictated by the Holy Spirit to the sacred authors.[48] Pope Leo XIII, in his famous encyclical on the study of Holy Scripture, declared: "For all the books which the Church receives as sacred and canonical are written wholly and entirely, with all their parts, at the dictation of the Holy Ghost. . . . This is the ancient and unchanging faith of the Church."[49] Therefore, while Masonry views Scripture as symbolic of the will of God, Christians believe it is indeed the word of God. "And," as Paul says, "we also thank God constantly for this, that when you received the word of God which you heard from us, you accepted it not as the word of men but as what it really is, the word of God, which is at work in you believers" (1 Thess 2:13).[50]

Just as Freemasonry views all gods as equal to Christ, the Lodge views all religious writings as equal to the Bible. The Masonic Service Association tells us: "Whether it be the Gospels

---

[48] See the Council of Trent, *Decree Concerning the Canonical Scriptures*, Session 4 (April 8, 1546); First Vatican Council, Session 3, Chapter 2, *On Revelation* (April 24, 1870), No. 5.

[49] Encyclical, *Providentissimus Deus* (November 18, 1893), No. 20.

[50] Because the Church teaches that God is the author of Scripture, the Bible is inerrant on all that it teaches. See, for example, Second Vatican Council, Dogmatic Constitution, *Dei Verbum* (November 18, 1965), No. 11; Pope Pius XII, *Divino Afflante Spiritu* (1943); Pope Benedict XV, *Spiritus Paraclitus* (1920); Pope Pius X, *Lamentabili Sane* (1907); Pope Leo XIII, *Providentissimus Deus* (1893); and Pope Pius IX, *Syllabus of Errors* (1864).

of the Christian, the Book of Law of the Hebrew, the Koran of the Mussulman, or the Vedas of the Hindu, it everywhere Masonically conveys the same idea — symbolizing the will of God revealed to man."[51] To Freemasonry, it doesn't matter that the Bible affirms the divinity of Christ while the Koran denies his divinity. For the Lodge, both views, however contradictory, are said to express the "will of God."

That religious writings found outside the Bible are not divinely inspired does not mean that they cannot assist in our search for God. The Church recognizes that other religious writings may nourish people in their relationship with God and even "reflect a ray of that truth which enlightens all men."[52] Other religious writings may thus serve to prepare God's people for the gospel message and predispose them to the truth of Jesus Christ. But unlike the Lodge's position, these writings can never be viewed as competing attempts to explain divine truth.

Because most lodges in the United States are made up of Christians and Jews, Christian Masons sometimes say that they have never participated in a lodge where books other than the Bible were displayed on the Masonic altar.[53] This may be true, but the argument does not address the problem of indifferentism that is promoted by the Lodge. If a lodge were to be visited by a regularly initiated Moslem who brought his copy of the Koran, by a Hindu who brought the Vedas, or by the Zoroastrian who brought the Zend Avesta, it would have to accommodate those writings

---

[51] *The Short Talk Bulletin*, "The Holy Bible," Vol. 2, No. 3 (1924).

[52] CDF, *Dominus Iesus*, No. 8; cf. CCC 2104.

[53] I always wondered why Jewish Masons seemed to have no problem with offering their Masonic worship around an altar displaying the New Testament. In fact, Jewish Masons invariably swear their Masonic oaths on Bibles that contain the New Testament. Their indifference is, perhaps, the fruit of their Masonic indoctrination.

on its altar, and Christian Masons would gather in worship around them. Through his tacit approval of indifferentism, the Christian Mason participates in profound religious error, offends the one true God, and injures the Body of Christ. He demonstrates his greater allegiance to the Lodge than to the truth, and weakens the Christian witness to those whom the Father also calls through his Son.

Final Thoughts

Many Christian Masons in this country never consider the issue of indifferentism. This is not surprising, since indifferentism seems to be the religion of America's pop culture. We live in a land of freedom and tolerance where equality is considered an absolute value. We are constantly conditioned to set aside our differences for the greater goal of mutual agreement. We are told to embrace the equality of ideas, not just the equality of persons. The Lodge can be very appealing to those who praise these ideals. The claim that there is only one way to heaven is often seen as intolerant and un-American. But if Christianity is going to be accused of intolerance, Christ himself must be similarly accused; it was he who declared himself the only way to the Father. While Christians declare that all men are equal, we emphatically proclaim that all religions are not.

Indifferentism is rarely addressed in the Sunday sermon, but it is a serious problem for the human family. This ideology is even more pernicious than an informed Protestant rejection of Catholic teaching. This is because the Protestant cares about the arguments. If he is presented the evidence of his error, he may be led to love the Church. The indifferentist, on the other hand, does not care about the arguments. Because he doesn't care, there is no error to recognize. The Lord Jesus warned us about being indifferent: "I know your works: you are neither cold nor hot. Would that you were cold or hot! So, because you are lukewarm, and neither cold nor hot, I will spew you out of my mouth" (Rev 3:15-16).

Ironically, though most Protestant churches have also condemned Freemasonry, indifferentism is the inevitable reaction to the rationalism of the Protestant Reformation. In interpreting the Bible, Protestant reformers elevated private judgment over the infallible teaching authority of the Catholic Church. Private judgment gave rise to modern indifferentism and continues to divide Protestantism into new sects each year. As divisions increase, Protestants attempt to find a principle of harmony in the theory that the essential doctrines of Christianity are contained in a few simple scriptural truths, and that whoever lives his life in accord with these truths is a faithful believer in Christ. Freemasonry dilutes the truth even further by espousing that the essential doctrines of God are contained in a few simple truths that human reason readily finds in the study of nature, and that whoever lives his life accordingly will enjoy eternal life with God. Protestants may have removed the living teaching authority of the Catholic Church, but Masons have removed Christ himself.

Chapter

IV

SPECIFIC MASONIC DOCTRINES AND PRACTICES

Overview of Masonic Syncretism

We have seen examples of how Freemasonry is indifferent to God's revelation, which has been perfectly completed in Jesus Christ. This section demonstrates how Masonry goes beyond indifferentism by formulating its own religious doctrines and practices. The Masonic Lodge's pursuit of creedal elements common to many religions results in a compromise known as syncretism. *Syncretism* is the blending of different beliefs or practices without regard for consistency, systematic connection, or compatibility with Christian truth. Syncretism is a logical consequence of indifferentism. If all religions are equally valid, then there is no problem with blending them together. Such a practice flows from a denial of the unique value of any one particular religion.

The Church has fought against syncretism throughout her history. Such instances included attempts to combine elements of Christianity with Judaism, Greek philosophy, Zoroastrianism, Buddhism, and ancient mystery religions. It was against the forces of syncretism that the Catholic Church developed her creeds and the canon of Scripture.

Masonry draws from many religions. As Masonic writer Manly P. Hall says, "A hundred religions have brought their gifts of wisdom to its altars."[1] Certainly, Freemasonry takes much from the world's three great religions. A good share of its practices is drawn from Christianity. The Bible is typically placed on the altar, and passages from the New Testament are woven into the rituals (though Christ is always omitted from the texts). Some lodges are even dedicated to St. John the Baptist and St. John the Evangelist, who are claimed as "eminent Christian patrons of Masonry."[2] Scottish Rite degrees even mirror the sacraments of the Eucharist (participants in white albs gather around an altar and consume hosts and wine) and confirmation (participants are anointed on their foreheads with chrism).

Masonry also draws extensively from Judaism. The setting for the three Masonic degrees is "King Solomon's Temple." The third degree, in particular, emphasizes many facets of Judaic worship, including the Sanctum Sanctorum, or Holy of Holies, and the Jewish law. Old Testament verses are read for each degree. The Entered Apprentice degree also calls to mind Israel's delivery from Pharaoh and the Egyptians by virtue of the miraculous departure through the parted Red Sea. During Holy Week, the Scottish Rite publicly celebrates what it calls the Feast of the Paschal Lamb, a commemoration of the Jewish Passover, which is celebrated with bread and wine.

Masonry also takes from Islam, particularly in the rituals of the Shrine. Shriners meet and perform their secret rituals in

---

[1] *An Encyclopedic Outline of Masonic, Hermetic, Qabbalistic, and Rosicrucian Symbolical Philosophy*, 176.

[2] Wisconsin Multiple Letter Cipher, 54. Masonry has appointed these feast days to celebrate the summer and winter pagan festivals of the sun.

"Mosques." Participants wear Islamic vestments and use symbolism such as the scimitar and crescent. Secret passwords of the Shrine are *Mecca* and *Medina*. The Shriner's oath is taken on the Koran and sworn to Allah.

In addition to the world's three principal religions, Freemasonry also draws from deism. In the Lodge, God is symbolized by an all-seeing eye and is given the deistic title of Great Architect of the Universe (discussed in the next section). Deism also asserts its right to perfect tolerance among all men, an overriding theme of the Lodge. Masonry draws from Gnosticism in its search for esoteric spiritual knowledge that is not available to the uninitiated. Masonry draws from rationalism in its lectures about knowing the existence of God through reason, and emphasizing the five basic human senses as the sources of knowledge. Masonry places emphasis on the spirituality and mysticism of the East as a source of wisdom and light. The Lodge also borrows from ancient pagan mystery religions, especially in the regeneration ceremony of the third degree (also discussed later). One can even see elements of Wicca and occultism in the Lodge's esoteric liturgies.[3] This is evident in the Masonic practice of appealing to the emotions of the candidate by blindfolding him, removing his clothing, intimidating him, and causing him to swear oaths under grisly penalties.

Much more could be said about the origins of the syncretistic practices of Freemasonry. The focus of this chapter, however,

---

[3] Bill Schnoebelen, a Protestant and former Freemason who spent seven years in the Church of Satan before giving his life to Christ in 1984, has spoken and written extensively about the similarities between Masonic and Satanic rituals. Anton LaVey, founder of the Church of Satan, makes reference to Freemasonry in his book *The Satanic Rituals: Companion to the Satanic Bible*. LaVey places particular emphasis on the ritual known as *L'Air Epais*, or the Ceremony of the Stifling Air. This ceremony uses extensive Masonic symbology and parallels the initiation rite enacted by the Ancient Arabic Order of Nobles of the Mystic Shrine (the "Shriners").

is the current doctrines and practices of American Masonry. These include Masonry's understanding and worship of God, its view of morality as the basis for salvation, its belief in the resurrection of the body, and its ceremonial burial rites that publicly present these doctrines. One finds these elements throughout Masonic ritual, the Masonic Bible, Masonic Landmarks, and in the publications of Masonic Grand Lodges and other recommended Masonic authorities. Let us begin by looking at Freemasonry's understanding of God.

Great Architect of the Universe

Freemasonry's understanding of God differs from that of Christianity. The Lodge sees God as the syncretistic Great Architect of the Universe who is worshiped in all religions, not the Triune God of the Father, the Son, and the Holy Spirit revealed in the Person of Jesus Christ. Past Grand Master Carl Claudy proclaims that all religious faiths lead to the Great Architect. "A hundred paths," he writes, "may wind upward around a mountain; at the top they meet."[4] Masonry's Great Architect of the Universe (GAOTU) is considered to be one God representing the deities of all religions. As the term is used, it requires that all deities are equal and that no particular faith or creed is unique. Although there is no consensus among Masons as to all the Landmarks, or unalterable principles, of Freemasonry, every list has included this belief in God as the Great Architect of the Universe, and every lodge in the United States uses this appellation.

The origin of the name GAOTU is Freemasonry's rationalistic belief that God definitively reveals himself only through the geometrical perfection of the universe. The Masonic Service Asso-

---

[4] *Introduction to Freemasonry*, Vol. 1, *Entered Apprentice*, 38.

ciation says that "Geometry . . . produces the nearest possible 'proof' of His existence."[5] Through geometry, the Mason is told, he can "discover the power, the wisdom, and the goodness of the Grand Artificer of the Universe, and view with delight the proportions which connect this vast machine."[6] Geometry is thus considered "the basis on which the superstructure of Masonry is erected."[7]

Because geometry is Masonry's best evidence of God's existence, God is symbolized in American and other English-speaking lodges by the capital letter *G*, standing, by Masonic tradition, for God, Geometry, and Gnosis. The letter *G* is typically suspended above the chair of the Worshipful Master, who presides in the eastern section of the lodge. This symbol, particular to no single system of belief, promotes Freemasonry's syncretistic understanding of deity. In fact, the Masonic Bible says that the letter *G* represents "the great God of all Freemasons" (p. 42). Before the letter *G*, the Mason is instructed, all created intelligence "should bow with reverence, most humbly bow."[8]

The intended result of using one symbol and a unique name for this representation is not only to unite men of various faiths into one spiritual brotherhood; it is also to unite the various deities of the different religions *into one spiritual godhead.* You cannot unite the worshipers without also uniting the worshiped. The Masonic Bible calls this the "unity of the Godhead" (p. 63). This syncretism renders the Triune God as nothing more than one of many components in this montage of deities. The Father, the Son, and the Holy Spirit become equal to Brahma, Vishnu, and Shiva in this composite godhead, and all Christian Masons are

---

[5] *The Short Talk Bulletin,* "Behind the Symbol," Vol. 32, No. 7 (1954).
[6] Wisconsin Multiple Letter Cipher (1998), 91.
[7] Ibid., 91.
[8] Ibid., 93.

instructed to bow in worship before the illuminated letter *G* that hangs majestically in the eastern quadrant of every Masonic lodge.

Chesterton, in his classic work *The Everlasting Man*, comments on how our distant relatives rejected the invitation to syncretism, which was a critical moment in history:

> The Theosophists built a pantheon . . . they call a Parliament of Religions. . . . Yet exactly such a pantheon had been set up two thousand years before by the shores of the Mediterranean; and Christians were invited to set up the image of Jesus side by side with the image of Jupiter, of Mithras, of Osiris, of Atys, or of Ammon. It was the refusal of the Christians that was the turning point in history. If the Christians had accepted, they and the whole world would have certainly, in a grotesque but exact metaphor, gone to pot. They would all have been boiled down in one lukewarm liquid in that great pot of cosmopolitan corruption in which all the other myths and mysteries were all ready melting. (p. 178)

What the Mediterranean world attempted to do two thousand years ago is no different than what the modern Masonic Lodge does today. Christian Masons are asked to place Christ alongside — not above — other gods. Just like the Romans of the ancient world, who were happy to absorb the gods of the conquered peoples while maintaining devotion to the gods of hearth and home, Christian Freemasons are to be content with praying to the Triune God on Sunday morning and to the Grand Artificer on Monday night. But Jesus said: "No one can serve two masters; for either he will hate the one and love the other, or he will be devoted to the one and despise the other. You cannot serve God and mammon" (Mt 6:24; cf. Lk 16:13).

Another of the Lodge's syncretistic symbols for God is the All-Seeing Eye. The meaning of the symbol has clear connections to

Enlightenment deism.[9] Deists, now commonly called "free thinkers," reject revealed truth and authoritative religious teaching in favor of purely rationalistic speculation about God (another reason Masonry calls itself "free" and "speculative"). Deism thinks of God as the divine watchmaker, the All-Seeing Eye who, having created a world, no longer takes an active part in its course. The All-Seeing Eye is displayed on many Masonic aprons, especially on those worn by former Worshipful Masters.

Henry Wilson Coil alludes to the pre-Christian origin of the "All-Seeing Eye," describing it as "a symbol of omnipresence and watchfulness of the Supreme Being," adding that the ancient Egyptians used the symbol to represent Osiris.[10] The Masonic Information Center further says that the symbol of the All-Seeing Eye was used, in ancient Egypt, to represent both God and King Osiris. The *Short Talk Bulletin* boasts that the All-Seeing Eye is a theme in Vedic hymns that predates Christianity by a thousand years.[11]

Freemasonry's use of GAOTU, the letter *G*, and the All-Seeing Eye goes beyond promoting a deistic understanding of God, even to embracing a polytheistic understanding of deity. This is needed because in the United States and most other countries, Freemasonry does not require its members to be monotheists. Being dogmatic about some particular conception of God would be considered un-Masonic because doing so would hamper Freemasonry's ability to bring together men of every creed and nation. Grand Lodges require only that members "believe in deity."

---

[9] See, for example, J. W. Acker, *Strange Altars: A Scriptural Appraisal of the Lodge*, 32.

[10] *Coil's Masonic Encyclopedia*, 27. Mackey also connects the All-Seeing Eye to Osiris in *Mackey's Revised Encyclopedia of Freemasonry*, Vol. 1, 52-53.

[11] *The Short Talk Bulletin*, "All-Seeing Eye," Vol. 10, No. 12 (1932).

Coil's Masonic Encyclopedia states that monotheism "violates Masonic principles, for it requires belief in a specific kind of Supreme Deity." Coil refers to the monotheistic God of Scripture as "a partisan, tribal God" and suggests that such a concept of God is inferior to the Lodge's, in which God is "a boundless, eternal, universal, undenominational, and international Divine Spirit, so vastly removed from the speck called man, that He cannot be known, named, or approached" (pp. 516-17). Albert Pike asserts that "every religion and every conception of God is idolatrous, insofar as it is imperfect, and as it substitutes a feeble and temporary idea in the shrine of that Undiscoverable Being [of Masonry]."[12] He notes that "every man's conception of God must be proportioned to his mental cultivation, and intellectual powers, and moral excellence," which makes of God "the reflected image of man himself."[13]

Freemasonry consequently invites believers of every stripe to gather under the canopy of the GAOTU. Oliver Street acknowledged the elasticity of the belief requirement when he stated that Masons could embrace "agnosticism, pantheism, nature religions and animism." Street wrote that sectarian religious beliefs could range "from the most refined and spiritual monotheism . . . to the basest form of nature worship, or of polytheism, or of fetishism and sorcery."[14]

In spite of the opinions of these prominent Masonic authorities, some Christian Masons insist that the "oneness" of the GAOTU requires monotheism and rejects polytheism, and on that ground alone, is a permissible characterization of God. The following statement from a Masonic source supports this position:

---

[12] *Morals and Dogma*, 516.
[13] Ibid., 234.
[14] "Freemasonry in Foreign Lands," *Little Masonic Library*, Vol. 1, 135.

"Monotheism is the sole dogma of Freemasonry. Belief in one God is required of every initiate, but his conception of the Supreme Being is left to his own interpretation. Freemasonry is not concerned with theological distinctions."[15]

Even if Grand Lodges were to require a belief in monotheism, this hardly mitigates the errors of Freemasonry. Masonry would still regard a deistic or unitarian understanding of God as a plausible alternative to the Trinity. Those who defend the monotheism of the Lodge must also contend with the fact that no Grand Lodge in the United States limits its membership to Jews, Moslems, and Christians. All men who believe in a supreme being are welcome into Masonry's hospitable bosom, including Hindus, Buddhists, and Shintoists. The Lodge's notion of God thus results in a common-denominator concept of deity even more syncretistic than would be a consolidation of the monotheistic beliefs of Christianity, Judaism, and Islam.

Claudy, in his popular work *Introduction to Freemasonry*, further explains that though the Mason is obliged to declare belief in some supreme being before being accepted, "he is not required to say, then or ever, *what* God. He may name him as he will, think of him as he pleases; make him impersonal law or personal and anthropomorphic; Freemasonry cares not."[16]

While Christian Masons believe it is permissible, even normative, to reduce the Blessed Trinity to a most generic expression of deity, the Church teaches that the Trinity is the "most fundamental and essential teaching in the hierarchy of the truths of faith. For Catholics, "the mystery of the Most Holy Trinity is the central mystery of Christian faith and life. It is the mystery of God in himself. It is therefore the source of all the other mysteries of

---

[15] Indiana Monitor (1975), 41.
[16] Vol. 1, *Entered Apprentice*, 109-10.

faith, the light that enlightens them" (CCC 234). For Christianity, the starting point for understanding the truth about God is the very mystery of the Trinity. For the Lodge, truth begins and ends with the GAOTU.

Therefore the Masonic understanding of God is in profound conflict with that of the Christian faith. The Christian God is not an umbrella deity under which all faiths can be found. He is unique and exclusive. He is One; he is also Triune. Supreme ruler of the universe, he is also Father, Son, and Holy Spirit. While he is Creator, he is also Redeemer and Sanctifier. While he can be known from the order of creation, he has also revealed himself in the Person of Jesus Christ.

Requiring a candidate for membership in an organization to believe in God may give the members a sense of unity and make them aware of the importance of God's presence in the organization's affairs. But an organization that requires a candidate to believe in God in order to get in the door is different from an organization whose entire focus is on God once he is inside. As the organization itself declares, "Everything in Masonry has reference to God, every lesson, every lecture, from the first step to the last degree. Without God it has no meaning, and no mission among men."[17] "God is the very warp and woof of Freemasonry," says Carl H. Claudy. "Take God out of Freemasonry and there is, literally, nothing left."[18]

Anglican theologian Dr. Hubert S. Box commented on Masonry's self-appointed teaching mission: "[T]o teach men about the nature of God is properly the responsibility of the church, by virtue of its divine commission." Box questions the right of "a rival teaching body having no divine commission to exercise such a

---

[17] *The Short Talk Bulletin*, "The Letter *G*," Vol. 5, No. 7 (1927).
[18] *Introduction to Freemasonry*, Vol. 2, *Fellowcraft*, 109.

function."[19] Any organization that introduces the concept of God into its formal teachings surely ought to say what it means by *God*. No matter how a Christian Mason views the GAOTU, we come to the same conclusion: in the lodge room, the Blessed Trinity is merely one of many equally plausible understandings of God, but in no way unique.

St. Paul reminds us that "although there may be so-called gods in heaven or on earth . . . yet for us there is one God, the Father, from whom are all things and for whom we exist, and one Lord, Jesus Christ, through whom are all things and through whom we exist" (1 Cor 8:5-6). David reveals that "all the gods of the peoples are idols; but the LORD made the heavens" (Ps 96:5). There is only one true God (of revelation), but many false gods (of men). We must therefore conclude that the GAOTU of the Masonic Lodge is the God of truth — *and error.* Such a god cannot be sought and worshiped by rational men.

Prayer and Worship

Freemasonry further promotes its syncretistic view of God through corporate prayer. Christians have been taught to call upon God the Father in the name of Jesus Christ (Jn 14:11, 13), but prayers in Masonic lodges are always directed to the Great Architect of the Universe (and other similar titles). The name of Jesus Christ is deliberately omitted from Masonic prayers. Mackey calls these omissions slight but necessary modifications.[20] Christian Masons thus argue that they can worship God outside of the church in a manner that would not be allowed inside the church. Of course, if omitting Jesus from prayers would be unacceptable to a Chris-

---

[19] *The Nature of Freemasonry*, 5.

[20] Cf. Albert Mackey, *Masonic Ritualist*, 272.

tian in a church, he cannot reasonably argue that such prayers somehow become complimentary in the lodge.

The most common prayer used by American Freemasons before any formal Masonic assembly illustrates this practice:

> Supreme Architect of the Universe, in Thy name we have assembled, and in Thy name we desire to proceed in all our doings. Grant that the sublime principles of Freemasonry may so subdue every discordant passion within us, so harmonize and enrich our hearts with Thine own love and goodness, that the lodge at this time may humbly reflect that beauty and order which reign forever before Thy Throne. Amen. So mote it be.[21]

Through the repeated use of these oral prayers, which are offered in an atmosphere of oath-bound secrecy, Christian Masons are conditioned to view God according to the Masonic worldview. The heavenly Father, whom the Son has revealed, thus becomes the God of any and every religious faith. The Masonic Service Association says that "Masonry invites to its altar men of all faiths, knowing that, if they use different names for the 'Nameless One of an hundred names,' they are yet praying to the one God and Father of all."[22]

While the Lodge is indifferent to the unique mediation of Christ (1 Tim 2:5-6), the Church teaches that "there is no other way of Christian prayer than Christ. Whether our prayer is communal or personal, vocal or interior, it has access to the Father only if we pray 'in the name' of Jesus" (CCC 2664). Omitting the name of Jesus from its worship is a necessary modification for the Lodge, but for the Christian, "the name 'Jesus' contains all: God

---

[21] Wisconsin Multiple Letter Cipher, 31-32.
[22] *The Short Talk Bulletin,* "The Holy Bible," Vol. 2, No. 3 (1924).

and man and the whole economy of creation and salvation" (CCC 2666).

Freemasonry's generic prayers to the GAOTU assume that God favorably responds to the prayers of those who reject his Son. Such a view is novel in the annals of Catholic thought. Prayer is a sacred and privileged form of interpersonal communion between God and those in covenant with him (cf. CCC 2564). Only those who are reborn in the waters of baptism enjoy this intimate, covenant relationship with God. The traditional teaching of the Church is that God hears the prayers of those outside his covenant only if it is a prayer of repentance for salvation.[23] God does not respond to the prayers of the unrighteous, especially for mundane and worldly favors such as his blessing upon the Masonic Lodge (cf. Jn 9:31; Ps 66:18; Prov 15:29; 28:9; Is 1:15).

Although grounded in the error of indifferentism, prayers and worship offered in the lodge are generally done with reverence. Few would question the seriousness of Freemasonry's ritualistic devotions to God. Most Grand Lodges do not even allow alcohol to be served on evenings when a degree is presented. But sincerity is not the aim of Christianity; *truth* is. When St. Paul traveled to Athens, he noticed how sincere the Greeks were in their worship of pagan deities. Everywhere Paul saw shrines and objects of their worship. He even noticed an altar with the inscription "To an unknown god" (Acts 17:23). But Paul did not let the Greeks on Mars Hill remain in ignorance. Paul boldly proclaimed: "What therefore you worship as unknown, this I proclaim to you" (v. 23).

After declaring the truth of Jesus Christ, Paul tells the Greeks that God formerly overlooked their ignorance. But now God commands all men to repent, "because he has fixed a day on which he

---

[23] See, for example, St. Thomas Aquinas, *Summa Theologica*, Question 83 (Of Prayer), Article 16.

will judge the world in righteousness by a man [Jesus] whom he has appointed . . . by raising him from the dead" (v. 31). In light of God's ensuing judgment, we must follow Paul's example by preaching Jesus' gospel of repentance and salvation to all men, not leaving them in their ignorance. One wonders what would have happened to the Athenians if Paul would have joined them in their worship of the "Nameless One of an hundred names," instead of proclaiming Jesus Christ, the name that is "above every name that is named, not only in this age but also in that which is to come" (Eph. 1:21). Certainly, many martyrdoms would have been avoided.

Approaching God in prayer as merely the "Great Architect of the Universe" also fosters a very impersonal view of God and robs him of his divine essence. "Designing the universe" is one of the things that God has done, *but it is not who God is.* Knowing "who God is" is essential to developing a personal relationship with him. God is a *Father*, first and foremost, and that is because he has a *Son*, Jesus Christ, whom he eternally begets in the Holy Spirit. God the Father invites us, not to marvel at his works from a distance, but to share intimately in the very life of his only Son. In baptism, we receive this gift of divine sonship and, with Christ, are able to cry "Abba, Father" (Rom 8:14-15; Gal 4:6; 3:26-27). Freemasonry does not approach God as Father in the Christian sense because Masonry denies God the Son: "No one who denies the Son has the Father. He who confesses the Son has the Father also" (1 Jn 2:23).

No matter how reverent his prayer in the Lodge, a Mason baptized in Christ cannot cultivate two relationships with God — one based on the interconfessionalism of the Lodge, and one based on the interior and sacramental life of the Church. If the Mason's goal is to grow in a deeper relationship with Christ, the practices of the Lodge cannot facilitate that goal. The Christian Mason cannot sincerely argue that reducing the name of the Blessed Trinity in prayer to the generic GAOTU helps him focus on Christ. If he does, he should equally admit that such a practice would bring the Hindu closer to Brahma. This begs the question why the Christian Mason would engage in a practice that encourages the worship of a false god. This is idolatry, which is a grave sin against God's First Commandment: "You shall have no other gods before me" (Deut 5:7).

Most Catholic Masons seem to have no problem with reducing the name of Jesus — the name above all names — to a common-denominator appellation in order to participate in worship with those who reject Christ. They often argue that such a practice allows men to pray together while putting their differences aside. But this argument assumes the overriding objective of corporate prayer is to achieve unity, even at the cost of obscuring the truth.

Such a compromise can never be a part of authentic Catholic prayer. The Church teaches that worship in common ("*communicatio in sacris*") is governed by the principle of bearing witness to the unity of the Church.[24] This is the sign our Lord prayed for to let the world know that he was indeed sent by the Father (cf. Jn 17:11, 21). By virtue of baptism, Jesus has allowed us to become part of his Mystical Body with a priestly office, so that whenever two or three gather in his name, he is present (cf. Mt 18:20; cf. CCC 2268). Corporate prayer is, thus, a visible sign of the "*Corpus Christi Mysticum*" that our Lord desires us to make manifest to the world.

Catholic participation in Masonic or any other non-Catholic worship that obscures this visible sign is a countersign, and prevents Catholic Masons from fully manifesting themselves as believers in Christ and members of his Body. This spiritual one-

---

[24] Cf. Second Vatican Council, *Unitatis Redintegratio* (November 21, 1964), No. 8.

ness that bears witness to the unity of the Church must be grounded in the fullness of truth that Jesus has revealed.

Masonic prayers, therefore, mix the sacred with the profane, and emphasize the brotherhood of the Lodge above truth. While brotherly love is essential to the Christian life, it must be rooted in Jesus Christ, the source of love and unity for God's human family. The commandments of loving God and our brother are profoundly connected. We reflect that love by sharing the light of Christ with others, and not hiding it: "Nor do men light a lamp and put it under a bushel, but on a stand, and it gives light to all in the house" (Mt 5:15; cf. Mk 4:21; Lk 8:16; 11:33).

Pope Pius XI reminds us that John, the apostle who ceaselessly taught us to "love one another," forbade any intercourse with those who professed a corrupt version of Christ's teaching (cf. 2 Jn 9-11).[25] Knowing the truth should mean sharing the truth, just as loving God should mean loving our neighbor. We can't do one without the other. Christian Masons cannot truly love their lodge brothers without bearing witness to the truth of Jesus Christ and his Catholic Church. Brotherly love without truth is like faith without works: it is dead (cf. Jas 2:17).

One can attribute Masonry's practice of prayer and worship to the current movement of Modernism, whose goal is to unite mankind in a spirit of reconciliation through feelings of the heart. This is done at the expense of doctrinal differences. But sound doctrine is a matter, not of feelings, but of truth. This setting aside of theological differences for the benefit of unified worship is the "false irenicism" the Church warns us about, in which the purity of Catholic doctrine becomes clouded.[26]

---

[25] Encyclical, *Mortalium Animos*, No. 9.

[26] Cf. Second Vatican Council, *Unitatis Redintegratio,* No. 11; cf. Pope Pius XII, *Humani Generis*, Nos. 11 and 12.

The practice of the Lodge raises the question of the efficacy of non-Christian prayer and worship, and whether Christians may ever participate in such activity. The Church acknowledges that some prayers and rituals of non-Christian religions may assume a role of preparation for the gospel in that through them, the human heart is prompted to be open to the action of God.[27] Indeed, God is willing to give his gift of the Holy Spirit to non-Christians who earnestly seek him (cf. Acts 10:45).[28]

It is not permissible, however, for Christians to participate in worship within the parameters of Masonry, in which non-Christian spiritualities are understood to be parallel or complementary to the unique mediation of Jesus Christ.[29] Prayer for the Christian must always be determined by the structure of the Christian faith, which bears witness to the truth. It should never be done in a forum that tempts the Christian Mason to lose sight of the conception of prayer as it has been revealed in Sacred Scripture.[30] Unlike the practice of the Lodge, prayer can "never be invoked to support religious relativism in the name of an experience that would lessen the value of God's revelation in history."[31] The Church is clear that the baptized, in order to avoid the "danger of falling into syncretism," must avoid the errors that "fuse Christian meditation with that which is non-Christian."[32]

---

[27] Cf. CDF, *Dominus Iesus*, No. 21; cf. CCC 843. See also Second Vatican Council, Dogmatic Constitution, *Lumen Gentium* (November 21, 1964), No. 62.

[28] Note that Cornelius was seeking the true God, not false gods. He "feared God" and "prayed constantly to God" (Acts 10:2). When he finally heard the gospel of Christ, he accepted it, and God responded by giving him the Holy Spirit (Acts 10:34-44). Cornelius is to be distinguished from those non-Christians who hear the gospel and reject it.

[29] Cf. Pope John Paul II, encyclical, *Redemptoris Missio*, No. 5.

[30] See Pope John Paul II, "Dialogue with the Great World Religions," *L'Osservatore Romano* (May 26, 1999), 7.

[31] Ibid.

[32] CDF, "Some Aspects of Christian Meditation" (October 15, 1989), No. 12.

As disciples of Christ, we feel the urgent need and the joy of witnessing to the fact that God manifested himself precisely in the Lord Jesus Christ. Therefore, our worship of God must bear witness to God's definitive revelation in Christ.[33] Participating in the common-denominator worship of Freemasonry not only weakens the Christian witness to others; it may even constitute an obstacle to salvation.[34]

Thus, living our baptismal faith and confessing the light of Jesus Christ before men is not just a matter of evangelization; *it is necessary for our salvation*. The Church teaches that "those who belong to Christ through faith and Baptism must confess their baptismal faith before men" (CCC 14). " 'All however must be prepared to confess Christ before men and to follow him along the way of the Cross, amidst the persecutions which the Church never lacks.' Service of and witness to the faith are necessary for salvation" (CCC 1816; cf. 2471). Jesus said, "So every one who acknowledges me before men, I also will acknowledge before my Father who is in heaven; but whoever denies me before men, I also will deny before my Father who is in heaven" (Mt 10:32; cf. Lk 12:8-9). Paul recognized this reality when he said, "Woe to me if I do not preach the gospel!" (1 Cor 9:16).

Because of the dangers of relativism and syncretism, Christians should avoid praying with nonbelievers, most especially on a regular and systematic basis as occurs in the lodge. Some argue that silent prayer would be more appropriate when both Christians and non-Christians are present. Silent prayer, however, would defeat the objectives of the Lodge. Through the use of its unique names, symbols, and oral petitions, Freemasonry seeks external and visible signs of unity among its members. When

---

[33] Cf. Ibid., "Dialogue with the Great World Religions," 7.
[34] Cf. CDF, *Dominus Iesus*, No. 21.

Masons bow in unison before the letter *G*, calling on the GAOTU with the same prayers around the same altar of Freemasonry, they are in pursuit of the common goal of *spiritual*, not fraternal, fellowship.

However, if two Masons do not agree on who God is, they lack spiritual unity. If Masons embrace entirely different pathways to God, they cannot be spiritually united. Even when the membership of a particular lodge is entirely Christian, Masonic prayer must nevertheless be offered in accordance with the universalism of the Brotherhood: "The universal nature of Masonry should never, under any circumstances, be forgotten or ignored, even if every member present is of the same religious belief . . . universality in Masonry means universality — all the time."[35]

Some argue that the Masonic practice of prayer and worship in the lodge is about being ecumenical and tolerant of others' religious beliefs. (*Ecumenism*, incidentally, is defined as promoting or tending toward worldwide Christian unity or cooperation. Thus it has nothing to do with non-Christian believers.[36]) This argument reveals a significant misunderstanding. The goal of ecumenism, and interreligious dialogue in general, is understanding, not agreement. True ecumenism and interreligious dialogue require not compromise, but honesty. Honesty promotes fruitful dialogue among the parties and, with respect to non-Christians, provides a forum for the proclamation of the gospel (which should be the *one and only goal* of ecumenism).[37]

Freemasonry has little to do with ecumenism and interreligious dialogue. Certainly, the Lodge's religious practices cannot compare with Christianity's ecumenical efforts, which seek to

---

[35] *Mentor's Manual, Grand Lodge of Indiana*, 75-76.

[36] Second Vatican Council, *Unitatis Redintegratio*, No. 1.

[37] See, for example, Pope Pius XI, *Mortalium Animos*, No. 10.

convert the world to Jesus Christ. The worship of the Lodge is also much more than an occasional gesture of goodwill. Freemasonry is a permanently established institution that claims to have the charism of enriching the spirituality of its members and advancing them to the celestial lodge above. The Lodge even claims that it is a "Divinely appointed institution,"[38] and that "no institution was ever raised on a better principle, or more solid foundation."[39]

The Lodge also does not encourage its members to practice their own religions. Although many Masons assume that the practice of their faith is encouraged by the Lodge, no such instruction exists in Masonic ritual. Masonry considers itself a completely self-sufficient system of religious and moral teaching whose members need nothing else to be spiritually edified, either in this life or the life to come: "These three degrees (1st, 2nd, 3rd) thus form a perfect and harmonious whole, nor can it be conceived that anything can be suggested more, which the soul of man requires."[40]

Freemasonry further prohibits the profession of any sectarian belief by the brothers in the lodge. It bans all interreligious dialogue. This prohibition is usually statutorily mandated — for example, "[A Grand Lodge] must exclude religious questions and discussions from its lodges."[41]

In light of this, lodges are correct in "forbidding all sectarian discussion within its lodge rooms."[42] Freemasonry therefore, precludes the opportunity for religious dialogue and tolerance in the

---

[38] See, for example, *Quarterly Bulletin of the Iowa Masonic Library* (1917), 54.

[39] Wisconsin Multiple Letter Cipher, 59.

[40] Daniel Sickles, *Ahimon Rezon; or, Freemason's Guide,* 196.

[41] *Wisconsin Masonic Code*, Section 37.03, Rule 4, Laws of the Grand Lodge (1997).

[42] Texas, *Monitor of the Lodge*, Monitorial Instructions in the Third Degree of Symbolic Freemasonry, 89.

lodge, and certainly any opportunity to bear witness to Christ. When a Mason states that Freemasonry is about religious tolerance, one might ask what is being tolerated, since its worship requires that the same names and symbols be used by everyone in the lodge room. Freemasonry encourages, not tolerance, but compromise because Freemasonry's goal is not understanding but agreement. Masonry wants to be the federation of religions, or the super-religion. Its aim is one common altar "at whose shrine the Hindoo, the Persian, the Assyrian, the Chaldean, the Egyptian, the Chinese, the Mohammedan, the Jew and the Christian may kneel."[43]

Any kind of pursuit of a spiritual unity of all peoples without Christ and his Church is diametrically opposed to God's plan of salvation. In fact, Scripture teaches that this is the work of the anti-Christ (see 2 Thess 2:3-4). The Church is "the visible plan of God's love for humanity," because God desires "that the whole human race may become one People of God, form one Body of Christ, and be built up into one temple of the Holy Spirit" (CCC 776). Therefore, the universal, or "catholic," spiritual unity that Freemasonry seeks, God has already given through his beloved Son Jesus Christ and his Holy Catholic Church.

System of Morality

Because Masonry does not bind itself to any sectarian creed, it has ample room to create its own teachings, not just about God but about morality as well. Freemasonry defines itself as "a peculiar system of morality, veiled in allegory, and illustrated by symbols."[44] No other benevolent fraternal order claims as much. But if

---

[43] Henry Pirtle, *The Kentucky Monitor* (1990), 95.
[44] Masonic Bible, 26.

Freemasonry truly can help mankind lead a morally better life, it is immoral to keep that knowledge to itself behind the secrecy of the lodge doors. If it does not have such knowledge, it is immoral to claim that it does.

As with its use of the word *truth*, Freemasonry loosely throws around the word *morality*. Having provided a relativistic definition of God, the Lodge's notion of morality is also relativistic. Allen E. Roberts, in his popular work *The Craft and Its Symbols*, argues in favor of a relativistic and subjective morality: "What is moral to one man may be immoral to another. Each man must decide for himself what the word encompasses, taking into account the moral standards of the society in which he lives. . . . He must set his own standards, his own principles" (p. 43). H. L. Haywood, in *The Great Teachings of Masonry*, offers a utilitarian view:

> Human experience, both individual and racial, is the one final authority on morality. . . . Wrong is whatever hurts human life, or destroys human happiness; right is whatever helps human life, and tends to sustain or increase human happiness. . . . Acts are not right or wrong intrinsically, but according as their effects are hurtful or helpful. (pp. 38-39)

Freemasonry emphasizes its peculiar system of morality throughout its rituals. The first-degree initiate is told before he enters the Lodge that Masonry consists of a course of moral instruction using ancient hieroglyphics. He is also told that through Masonry he will build his "future moral and Masonic edifice."[45] Masonry further inculcates its system of morality through the use of Masonic symbols such as the Square, which it considers an emblem of morality and one of the tools of a Mason's profession. The Compasses are said to contain the most excellent

---

[45] Wisconsin Multiple Letter Cipher, 49.

tenets of the Order: morality, friendship, and brotherly love. Finally, Masons pray in their lodges that every moral and social virtue should unite and cement them.

Since American Masonic lodges are predominantly Christian and Jewish, one would suppose that the Craft would, at a minimum, make reference to the Ten Commandments in its moral teachings. Nonetheless, Masonic ritual makes no reference to them. Why? Because they are part of God's divine revelation. Therefore, while most Masons would presumably agree on the grave obligations set forth in the Decalogue, Freemasonry's system of morality must exclude them from its nonsectarian theology.

The Church, however, tells us that if moral teaching is divorced from God's revealed truth, observance of the moral law will be severely impeded. This is because our discernment of the moral law is tainted by original sin. "In the present situation sinful man needs grace and revelation so moral and religious truths may be known 'by everyone with facility, with firm certainty and with no admixture of error' " (CCC 1960). Because our vision of the moral law is often obscured and coupled with temptations to transgress it, a system of morality needs to be grounded in religious truth. That truth is the gospel of Jesus Christ.[46] Christians cannot separate the truth of Christ from the moral law because "the moral law finds its fullness and its unity in Christ" (CCC 1953).

Because Freemasonry's system of morality is indifferent to God's grace and revelation, it has separated Christ from the moral law. Its teachings therefore deviate from those of the gospel. For example, Freemasonry teaches its members that other Freemasons should be the special object of their charity and puts Masonic relatives in a special class. The Mason is instructed to "circumscribe and keep yourself within due bounds with all mankind, *more*

---

[46] Second Vatican Council, *Dei Verbum*, No. 7.

especially with a brother Mason."[47] The Mason is also told that "should you ever meet a member of the human family, *especially a brother Mason*, in a like destitute situation, it would be your duty to contribute to his relief as liberally as his necessities might require, and your ability permits."[48] Masons are taught that because they are Masons, they have a greater duty than others to be charitable toward others: "To relieve the distressed is a duty incumbent on all men, *but more particularly on Masons*, who are linked together by an indissoluble chain of sincere affection."[49]

The Lodge also requires the Mason to swear to God to "help, aid, and assist all poor and distressed Master Masons, their widows and orphans, they applying to me as such, I finding them worthy, and can do so without material injury to myself or family."[50] The immorality of such an oath is addressed in Chapter V. But the Lodge's limitations on Masonic charity (the person's need and the Mason's ability) differ from the charity of the gospel, as we see in the stories of the poor widow (Mk 12:42-43; Lk 21:2-3), the rich man seeking perfection (Lk 18:18-24), and that greatest gift of all: laying one's life down for another (Jn 15:13; 1 Jn 3:16).

Speaking of Masonic charity, Freemasonry's charitable works have been publicly criticized. The *Orlando Sentinel* published that the Shrine generated $23 million in 1985 from its circuses through the country, but its tax returns showed less than two percent (or $346,251) actually went to medical care for children. The rest of the money was used to furnish the Shrine's elaborate temples and to purchase food, alcohol, and costumes for its rituals (August 3 and 7, 1985; September 15, 1985). Ann Landers also reported this activity in the article "Shrine Records Shocking" (*South Haven Daily*

---

[47] Wisconsin Multiple Letter Cipher, 41.
[48] Nevada Ritual, 27.
[49] Wisconsin Multiple Letter Cipher, 55 (emphases added).
[50] Nevada Ritual, 120.

Tribune [Michigan]; April 24, 1987). Many Grand Lodges throughout the United States have also accumulated significant wealth. When I left Freemasonry, the Grand Lodge of Wisconsin had over $11 million in the bank, none of which was earmarked for charity. This amount did not include its ownership value (also worth millions) in the approximately two hundred fifty Blue lodges in the state (all Grand Lodges own the assets of their subsidiary lodges). Other Grand Lodges enjoy similar wealth.

A Mason is also required to swear to God that he "will not have illicit carnal intercourse with a Master Mason's wife, mother, sister or daughter."[51] A man who commits such an act violates his Masonic oath and risks expulsion. But there is no such sanction for carnal intercourse with non-Masonically affiliated women. While such an act of fornication or adultery would be equally sinful, Freemasonry seems to suggest one offense is graver than the other, and that is gravely offensive from a Christian perspective.

The Mason is also required to swear that he will "keep the secrets of a brother Master Mason inviolate, when communicated to and received by [him] as such, murder and treason excluded."[52] Edmund Ronayne's *Handbook of Freemasonry*, for example, instructs Masons: "You must conceal all crimes of your brother Masons . . . and should you be summoned as a witness against a brother Mason be always sure to shield him. . . . It may be perjury to do this, it is true, but you're keeping your obligations" (p. 183). Thus, Masonry's system of morality condones bearing false witness against another, which is a violation of the moral law.

While Freemasonry acknowledges that we are all part of the human family, its system of morality demands special treatment for Freemasons under the solemn obligation of an oath. When a Mason must choose between another Mason and a "profane" (one

---

[51] Wisconsin Multiple Letter Cipher, 113.
[52] Ibid.

not initiated into the mysteries of Freemasonry), he is oath-bound to his brother Mason. But our Lord commands that we "love our neighbors as ourselves" and love even our enemies, "to make ourselves the neighbor of those farthest away" (CCC 1825; cf. Mt 5:44; Lk 6:27, 35).

Freemasonry's requirements for admission into its system of morality also do not comport with Christian moral principles. In addition to denying membership to females and children, Freemasonry commonly rejects petitions from men who have mental or physical handicaps. This is another "Landmark" of Freemasonry. The Masonic Bible (p. 29) requires that a candidate "must be a man, free born, of lawful age, sound in body and limb, and not in his dotage; mentally, he must be intelligent, capable of comprehending the profound truths and tenets of the Order." My Grand Lodge's law read: "A lodge shall not receive a petition for the degrees from one who cannot read or write, nor from one who is unable to speak and understand the language of the ritual."[53]

Masonry requires its members to have no mental or physical defects for several reasons. A candidate must be able to swear the secret Masonic oaths. Since the oath is what formally binds a man to Freemasonry, he must be able to speak and understand it. Also, while taking his oath, the candidate is required to position his hands and feet in a particular way as he kneels at the Masonic altar. Throughout Masonic ritual and at every lodge meeting, Masons are also required to make secret signs of self-mutilation with their arms and hands. These signs evoke the penalties for breaking the Masonic oaths and constantly remind the Mason of his sacred tie to Freemasonry. If a man is physically or psychologically challenged and cannot perform these gestures, he is not allowed into Freemasonry's system of morality.

---

[53] *Wisconsin Masonic Code*, Section 66.04, Regulations for Lodges (1997).

Freemasonry has historically not recognized Masonic lodges organized by black Masons. While white Masons often contend that this is due to technicalities concerning jurisdiction, the primary reason appears to be prejudice. Prince Hall, considered the Father of black Masonry in the United States, and fourteen other black men were initiated Masons in a universally recognized military lodge in Boston, in 1775. In 1784, Prince Hall received a charter from the Grand Lodge of England to form an African-American lodge, recognizing it as a valid and universal American Masonic Lodge. Notwithstanding Prince Hall's legitimacy, American Grand Lodges have historically been reluctant to recognize black lodges or invite African-Americans into Freemasonry's system of morality. Freemasonry's prejudice against black Masons has slowly diminished over time, but still only about one half of United States Grand Lodges recognize Prince Hall Grand Lodges as regular Masonry. Today Prince Hall has over forty-five hundred Masonic lodges worldwide with approximately three hundred thousand Masons.

Freemasonry is no stranger to racism. Most of the major leaders of the Ku Klux Klan were Masons. Confederate General Nathan Bedford Forrest, the founder of the Klan and its first Imperial Wizard, was a Freemason. Colonel William J. Simmons, who in 1915 reestablished the Klan at Atlanta, where he became Imperial Wizard, was a Mason and a Knight Templar. Dr. Hiram Evans, who succeeded Colonel Simmons as Imperial Wizard, was a 32nd-degree Mason. Albert Pike held the office of Chief Justice of the Ku Klux Klan at the same time as he was the Sovereign Grand Commander of the Scottish Rite, Southern Jurisdiction. Many believe Pike devised the secret oaths of the Klan, whose bloodcurdling penalties are very similar to those used in Masonry. Supreme Court Justice Hugo Black, whom we learn more about in Chapter VIII, was also a Klansman and a 33rd-degree Mason.

Masonry's system of morality goes beyond providing instructions for the present life; it promises rewards in the next. The Masonic Service Association teaches that Masonry is not just a ritual but a way of living: "It offers us a plan, a method, a faith by which we may build our days and years into a character so strong and true that nothing, not even death, can destroy it."[54]

Man is viewed by the Lodge, not as a sinner in need of God's grace, but as a "spiritual temple" that the good Mason continues to build and perfect so as to merit eternal life. The Masonic Bible (p. 56) calls the building of this spiritual edifice the "supreme end of Freemasonry." Hence we have the term "Speculative Masonry," which refers to the construction of this spiritual temple: the soul of the individual Mason. The Lodge contrasts this symbolism with "Operative Masonry," which refers to the building of physical structures, specifically, King Solomon's Temple. The Masonic Bible explains: "Some of the most sublime symbolisms of Freemasonry relate to the building of this spiritual temple under the principles and tenets of Freemasonry, based upon the building of Solomon's Temple by Operative Masons" (p. 58).

The Mason is instructed to devote himself to becoming worthy of heaven:

> Let all the energies of our souls and the perfection of our minds be employed in attaining the approbation of the Grand Master on high, so that when we come to die, . . . we gain the favor of a speedy entrance to the Grand Lodge on high where the G.A. of T.U. forever presides, and where, seated at his right hand, he may be pleased to pronounce us upright men and Masons.[55]

---

[54] *The Short Talk Bulletin*, "The Square," Vol. 2, No. 4 (1924).
[55] George Simmons and Robert Macoy, *Standard Masonic Monitor of the Degrees of Entered Apprentice, Fellow Craft, and Master Mason,* 125.

The Entered Apprentice Mason is called a "Rough Ashlar," meaning a stone taken from the quarry in its rude, natural state. Without any discussion of the stain of original sin or the need for baptism, the Lodge teaches its members that they can, by their own works, become Perfect Ashlars. A Perfect Ashlar symbolizes a state of perfection before God. This transformation, the Lodge teaches, can all be gleaned from "the great book of nature and revelation."

To reach the desired state of perfection, the Entered Apprentice Mason is presented with a Common Gavel, "an instrument made use of by operative medieval Masons to break off the rough and superfluous parts of stones, the better to fit them for the builder's use;" but Freemasons are told to make use of it "for the more noble and glorious purpose of divesting [their] minds and consciences of all the vices and superfluities of life."[56] It is the Mason's good conduct, independent of God's gifts of grace and mercy, that is to make him fit for the "house not made with hands, eternal in the heavens."[57] As the Entered Apprentice is presented with a Masonic lambskin apron, he receives this reminder:

> The lamb has in all ages been deemed an emblem of innocence; he, therefore, who wears the lambskin as a badge of Masonry is thereby continually reminded of that purity of life and conduct, which is essentially necessary to his gaining admission into the Celestial Lodge above, where the Supreme Architect of the Universe presides."[58]

The Mason is also told that he will never again receive such a distinguished honor as the Masonic apron this side of heaven: "But never again from mortal hands — never again until your

[56] Grand Lodge of Texas, Monitor of the Lodge, 19.
[57] Texas, Monitor of the Lodge, 19; see also Masonic Bible, 35.
[58] Minnesota, Masonic Manual, 20. The apron, called "the badge of a Mason," is worn around the waist at all official Masonic gatherings.

enfranchised spirit shall have passed upward and inward through the pearly gates shall any honor so distinguished, so emblematical of purity and of all perfection, be bestowed upon you, as this which I now confer."[59] He is taught that wearing this emblem of perfection will help secure God's favorable judgment after he dies, as his "trembling soul stands naked and alone before the Great White Throne."[60] (It is interesting to note that, in Scripture, the "Great White Throne" refers exclusively to the throne that God will sit upon when he condemns the unrighteous to hell; see Rev 20:11-15).

The Master Mason degree offers its recipients further spiritual consolations: "That All-Seeing Eye, whom the sun, moon and stars obey, and under whose watchful care even Comets perform their stupendous revolutions, pervades the inmost recesses of the human heart and will reward us according to our merits"[61] — and, "as Master Masons, we may enjoy the happy reflections consequent on a well-spent life, and die in the hope of a glorious immortality."[62] The Masonic Bible affirms the certainty of the Mason's eternal fate: ". . . when this earthly tabernacle of his shall have passed away, he has within him a sure foundation of eternal life, a cornerstone of immortality emanating from the Divine Spirit, and which will survive the tomb, returning to his Creator and God, above the decaying dust of mortality and the grave" (p. 38).

The building of the spiritual temple, in the Lodge's system of morality, thus is not just a matter of living a moral life; it is a way of earning the reward of heaven. Through the symbolism of the Rough Ashlar, the Common Gavel, and the Masonic apron, Freemasonry makes a statement on what it believes is necessary to

---

[59] Wisconsin Multiple Letter Cipher, 195.

[60] Ibid., 196.

[61] Minnesota, Masonic Manual, 53, 55.

[62] Ibid., 53.

gain admission into heaven: a Mason's good conduct, *no matter what religion he professes*. In other words, Freemasonry teaches that Masons make themselves fit before God and gain eternal life by their own works, *independent* of God's grace through faith in Jesus Christ. Masonry thus identifies religion with morality while ignoring the theological differences of its members. This moralization of religion renders Christianity nothing more than a system of ethical behavior useful for helping one lead a better life, instead of the exclusive means by which God in his mercy calls us to eternal life in his only-begotten Son.

Freemasonry's teachings on how a Mason makes himself fit for heaven are in profound conflict with the Christian faith. All men, prior to repentance and baptism, are under the full curse of eternal death for their sins. They are born under the condemnation "of the law" (cf. Rom 4:15; Gal 3:10). There is absolutely nothing a man can do by his own efforts to merit eternal life (whether it be faith or works). It is only when a man responds to God's actual grace that the judgment of the law is removed. The great Council of Trent dogmatically proclaimed: "If anyone says that man can be justified before God by his own works, whether done by his own natural powers or through the teaching of the law, without divine grace through Jesus Christ, let him be anathema."[63]

The Church teaches that a man's correct response to God's *actual grace* is to repent of his sins and be baptized in Christ. When he so responds, God removes him from the condemnation of the law and man enters into the system of grace (cf. Rom 5:1-2). In baptism, God forgives man his sins, infuses his soul with *sanctifying grace*, and the man becomes a child of God (cf. Titus 3:5-7). Man is then able to have a gracious relationship with God, and God will reward him for his faith and works (not because God is

---

[63] Session 6, Canon 1 on Justification.

obligated, but because it is his nature to reward his children). If man does not respond to God's grace in Christ, he remains under God's condemnation in the system of law and can have no hope of eternal life (cf. CCC 679). Jesus made this clear when he said: "He who believes in him is not condemned; he who does not believe is condemned *already*, because he has not believed in the name of the only Son of God" (Jn 3:18; emphasis added).

Because man cannot have any favor before God until he responds to God's grace, the Church has always taught that God makes the first move:

> The merit of man before God in the Christian life arises from the fact that *God has freely chosen to associate man with the work of his grace.* The fatherly action of God is first on his own initiative, and then follows man's free acting through his collaboration, so that the merit of good works is to be attributed in the first place to the grace of God, then to the faithful. (CCC 2008; emphasis in original.)

Since, in the order of grace, the initiative belongs to God, "*no one can merit the initial grace* of forgiveness and justification" (CCC 2010; emphasis in original). Because of the immeasurable inequality between God and his creatures, there is no strict right to any merit on the part of man, no matter how "good" he is (cf. CCC 2007).

Why is God able to offer man grace to save his soul? Because of the Passion of Jesus Christ, who offered himself on the cross as a living victim, holy and pleasing to God, and whose blood has become the instrument of atonement for the sins of all men (cf. CCC 1992). Grace is *favor*, not earned by the Mason's efforts of living a life of Masonic virtue, but given freely and undeservedly by God through Christ to help us respond to his call to become children of God, adoptive sons, partakers of the divine nature and of eternal life (cf. CCC 1996). While the Lodge teaches its members that the All-Seeing Eye will reward them according to their merits, it fails to mention that all merits before God come solely from the charity of Jesus Christ (cf. CCC 2011).

Because Freemasonry does not acknowledge our need for grace as it teaches about attaining perfection, there is no mention of our call to sanctification and holiness, which is Christian perfection, the aim of our earthly life. To be pleasing to God, we must become holy as he is holy. In Leviticus 19:2, we read, "You shall be holy; for I the LORD your God am holy." God calls each of us to this perfection in holiness (cf. CCC 2013). The perfection to which we are called comes, not by way of the Common Gavel, but by way of the cross (cf. CCC 2015). "If any man would come after me," says Jesus, "let him deny himself and take up his cross and follow me" (Mt 16:24; cf. Mk 8:34; Lk 9:23). There is no holiness without renunciation and spiritual battle (cf. 2 Tim 2:3; Col 1:24). Since holiness is the work of God's grace, which escapes our experience, we cannot, despite what is taught by the Lodge, rely on our feelings or our works to conclude that we are justified and saved (cf. CCC 2005). We cannot be assured that our efforts "will pass the test of the great Master Builder of heaven" (Masonic Bible, p. 50).

Even on the natural level, we recognize our weakness of character and our inclination toward sin. The Church calls this inclination "concupiscence." Our concupiscence inclines us to earthly pleasures in a manner that is contrary to the dictates of reason (cf. CCC 405, 418, 1264, 1426). We need God's grace in order to overcome these disordered passions. Sin is too deeply ingrained to be smoothed over with the Common Gavel of our own efforts. While Masonry does not expressly reject the truths of sin and grace in its rituals, it holds these doctrines to be matters of indifference. Such a view is equally hostile to the Christian faith and harmful to souls.

Freemasonry's teachings about obtaining eternal life are reminiscent of the inevitable errors of private-judgment theology vis-à-vis the teaching authority of the Catholic Church. Martin Luther's rejection of the Church's fifteen-hundred-year-old teaching regarding the necessity of both faith and works in God's plan of salvation has led to innumerable divisions within Protestantism. One can see the connection between Luther's "Salvation by faith alone" and Freemasonry's doctrine of "Salvation by works alone." Luther essentially said, "Believe right, and I care not what you do." Freemasonry says, "Do right, and we care not what you believe."

Resurrection of the Body

As mentioned in Chapter II, even though there are Masonic degrees numerically higher than the third degree (for example, the 32nd degree of the Scottish Rite), the third, or Master Mason's, degree is considered Freemasonry's pinnacle. It is the third degree that teaches the most sublime of all Masonic beliefs: the resurrection of the body and the immortality of the soul. All of the instruction the Mason has received to this point concerning the building of his moral and spiritual edifice culminates in this degree. The Masonic Bible states: "The doctrine of the resurrection of the body to a future and eternal life constitutes an essential dogma of the religious faith of Freemasonry. It is more authoritatively inculcated in the symbolism of the Third Degree than is possible by any dogmatic creed" (p. 55). As with the GAOTU, the Masonic belief in a resurrection to a future life is one of the Landmarks of Freemasonry. Mackey's twentieth Landmark states that "[t]o believe in Masonry, and not to believe in a resurrection, would be an absurd anomaly."[64]

---

[64] "The Landmarks, or the Unwritten Law," *Little Masonic Library*, Vol. 1, 55.

Like so many of the Lodge's teachings, the doctrine of the resurrection is conveyed through symbolism. But unlike other teachings, in which symbols are presented to the candidate with a brief explanation of their meaning, belief in the resurrection is taught by an extensive allegorical drama in which the candidate, to his surprise, actively participates. The Masonic Bible (p. 63) defines an allegory as "uttering a truth in parabolic form, with its meaning hidden in comparison." The drama, called "the Legend of the Third Degree" or "the Hiramic Legend," is considered "the most important and significant of the legendary symbols of Freemasonry."[65]

The Legend of the Third Degree has been a part of modern Freemasonry since about 1723. Like the doctrine it exemplifies, it is considered a Landmark of the Craft. Should any rite either exclude the Hiramic Legend or substantially alter it, that rite would "cease to be a Masonic rite."[66]

Before the Hiramic Legend commences, the Master Mason degree proceeds in a fashion similar to that of the Entered Apprentice and Fellowcraft degrees (Masonic initiation is discussed in Chapter V). The candidate is divested of all his clothing except his underwear, and conducted blindfolded into the lodge room. There he swears an oath of loyalty to Masonry — on the Holy Bible if he is a Christian — under symbolic penalties of physical torture and death. The blindfold is then removed, and the brother is given the secret signs, password, and grips of a Master Mason. Following a brief instruction concerning the symbolism of the degree, the Mason is conducted out of the lodge to get dressed again, and the meeting is adjourned (the meeting is called "from labor to refreshment").

---

[65] Indiana Monitor, 41.
[66] Little Masonic Library, 49.

The candidate, now fully dressed, is adorned with the Jewel of the Junior Warden as a token of his accomplishments. The meeting resumes and the candidate is seated on the sidelines with the rest of his brethren, clothed for the first time in the apron of a Master Mason. Having just sworn the oath, the candidate believes he is now a full-fledged Master Mason. However, to the candidate's surprise, the Worshipful Master summons him to the front of the lodge room to tell him that he is not yet a Master Mason. There is yet a rugged path to travel, beset with ruffians and murderers. He is warned that he may even lose his life, but "he that endures to the end, the same shall be saved."

The candidate then participates in a drama in which he plays a character named Hiram Abif, the master workman on King Solomon's Temple.[67] Hiram is understood to have the secret "Word" of a Master Mason, symbolic of divine knowledge, or the real name of God. In preparation for his journey, the candidate is blindfolded again and escorted to the Masonic altar. There he is asked to kneel and pray, mentally or orally, as he pleases. When finished, he is to say "Amen." Then the Hiramic Legend begins.

The Senior Deacon helps the candidate rise from the altar and escorts him around the lodge room, explaining that it was Hiram Abif's custom during the construction of King Solomon's Temple to enter the unfinished Sanctum Sanctorum and offer his devotions to deity. Afterward, he would retire by the South Gate. Therefore, in imitation of this ancient custom, the Senior Deacon informs the candidate that he will also retire by the South Gate.

As the Senior Deacon leads the blindfolded candidate around the room, he is stopped by three ruffians, one after another. The ruffians are said to be Fellowcrafts, previously working under

---

[67] Hiram Abif is mentioned in 1 Kings 7:13-14; 2 Chron 2:14; 4:16.

Hiram Abif at King Solomon's Temple, who have entered into a conspiracy to extort Masonic secrets from Hiram Abif. Jubela, the first ruffian, who is positioned at the South Gate, demands of Hiram the secrets of a Master Mason, or Master's Word. (Each ruffian pushes the candidate around a little, grabbing his shirt, and so forth.) The Senior Deacon answers for the blindfolded candidate, saying that he would never divulge the secrets. Jubela then gives the candidate a gentle blow on the neck with a Masonic tool called a twenty-four-inch gauge. The Senior Deacon quickly leads the candidate away in escape.

A few moments later, Jubelo, the second ruffian, positioned at the West Gate, stops Hiram, and makes the same demands. Hiram refuses. Jubelo then gives the candidate a soft blow on the chest with a carpenter's square, and Hiram escapes again.

As the Senior Deacon hurries the candidate away, Hiram is confronted by the third ruffian, Jubelum, who warns Hiram that this time he will not escape. He informs Hiram that he has an instrument of death, and should Hiram refuse to divulge the secrets of a Master Mason, he will die. As in the first two confrontations, Hiram refuses. Jubelum then gives the blindfolded candidate the "death blow," hitting him over the head with a setting maul, or padded mallet. Knocked off his feet and caught in a large sack by the brethren, he is instructed to remain lying on the floor.

As Hiram lies "dead" in the Temple, the ruffians recognize the horrid deed they have done. They have murdered their Grand Master Hiram Abif. Because of the hour (it is "high twelve"), the ruffians, fearing discovery, bury the body in the rubbish of the Temple and agree to meet at "low twelve" the next day to give the body a proper burial. The candidate is symbolically buried (the brethren throw scraps of wood or other materials over the candidate's body).

After a period of silence, a bell tolls twelve times and the ruffians reconvene. They take the body out from the rubbish and
bury it on the brow of a hill, west of Mount Moriah. The ruffians
decide to plant a sprig of acacia next to the head of the grave in
order to conceal it and to identify the burial place should that ever
be required. They then attempt to make their escape.

Back at the Temple, King Solomon, learning of Hiram Abif's
absence, dispatches a search party of Fellowcrafts. After many days,
one of the weary Fellowcrafts decides to rest on the brow of the
very hill where Hiram is buried. On rising, he grabs hold of the
acacia plant, which gives way. The Masonic Bible (p. 43) says that
the acacia is "to teach symbolically the great Masonic doctrine of
a resurrection and future life."

The Fellowcraft shows his comrades the loose acacia and the
fresh grave. Upon this discovery, the Fellowcrafts hear through the
clefts of the rocks the three ruffians lamenting over their deeds
and crying out the penalties of their Masonic oaths. The Fellowcrafts rush to arrest the ruffians and take them back to King
Solomon, where they are tried for murder. King Solomon orders
their execution according to the penalties of their Masonic oaths.
King Solomon then orders the Fellowcrafts to go in search of
Hiram's body and, if found, to observe whether the Master's Word,
a key to it, or anything appertaining to the Master's Degree can be
found on or about it. The Fellowcrafts return to the site where
they found the acacia, open the grave, and discover Hiram's rot-
ting corpse. He is identified by the Jewel of the Junior Warden
around his neck. (The candidate's blindfold is now removed.) The
Fellowcrafts return the Jewel to King Solomon, who confirms that
it indeed belonged to Hiram Abif. He then orders a procession to
the grave, during which a funeral dirge may be sung.

At the gravesite, the brethren form a circle, holding their hands
out over the body, positioned as when they took the Master Mason

oath on the Bible. When the Masons have circled the grave, they raise their arms above their heads in horror and surprise, crying out, "Oh, Lord, my God, is there no help for the widow's son?" (Known as the "Great [or Grand] Hailing Sign of Distress," this secret mode of recognition is used by a Master Mason to communicate to another Master Mason that he is in danger.)

After these exclamations, King Solomon orders one of the Fellowcrafts to raise the body by means of the Entered Apprentice grip; but the flesh slips from the bone, and the body cannot be raised. Then King Solomon orders another Fellowcraft to raise the body by the Fellowcraft grip; but for the same reason, it cannot be done. At this point, the brothers kneel around the grave, and the Worshipful Master, who plays King Solomon, or the Senior Warden, who plays King Hiram of Tyre, leads all those present in a prayer of "everlasting salvation" for the fallen martyr.[68]

After the prayer, King Solomon, portrayed by the Worshipful Master, declares that the body will now be raised. He then raises the body to a standing position by the strong grip of a Master Mason, or Lion's Paw (often called raising the candidate from "a dead level to a living perpendicular"). The standing position to which the candidate is raised is called "the five points of fellowship" because he is foot-to-foot, knee-to-knee, breast-to-breast, hand-to-back, and cheek-to-cheek or mouth-to-ear with the Worshipful Master. These five points represent various Masonic virtues that will later be explained to him. Immediately after the candidate is raised to the proper position, the Worshipful Master whispers the Grand Masonic Word, "Ma-Ha-Bone," into his ear and instructs the newly made Master Mason to whisper the same back to him.

The Masonic Bible defines this process of raising the candidate as follows: "Literally, this refers to a portion of the ceremony;

---

[68] Nevada Ritual, 137.

but more significantly, it refers symbolically to the resurrection, which is exemplified as the object of the degree" (p. 55). *Mackey's Revised Encyclopedia of Freemasonry* describes the symbolism of the "raising" the same way (vol. 2, p. 828). Right after the Mason is raised, he is given a lecture that articulates the meaning of the Hiramic Legend and, thus, of the third degree. That meaning is a testament to Masonry's "faith in the resurrection of the body and the immortality of the soul."[69] The lecture concludes with an exhortation to the brethren who are present. They are to imitate Hiram Abif's piety and fidelity so that at life's end they may be "translated" from this imperfect world to the heavenly Lodge above, where they will abide with the Great Architect of the Universe.[70]

Once the veil of this allegorical drama is lifted, one can only conclude that the Mason, without forewarning, has just been reborn ("raised") into a new religious faith through symbolic death, burial, and resurrection.

Following the lecture explaining the degree, the Master Mason is presented with a Masonic Bible. The Masonic Bible, which I cite throughout this book, offers further catechesis on Freemasonry's belief in the resurrection of the body:

- "A distinctive tenet of Masonry is that there remains a heaven of rest and of rewards for the good and faithful, a place of perfect happiness beyond the grave and the resurrection of the body" (p. 44).
- "The doctrine of eternal life permeates all the Mysteries of Freemasonry; it is the fundamental basis of the Third Degree in a very special emphasis. Co-equal with emphasis on this tenet of Masonic Faith is belief in the future resurrection of the body" (p. 41).

---

[69] Wisconsin Multiple Letter Cipher, 136.
[70] Arkansas, *Masonic Monitor*, 68.

- "Foremost of all the truths taught and emphasized in [the Master Mason] degree, is the immortality of the soul of man and the certainty of the resurrection of his body to eternal life" (p. 11).
- ". . . there will be an awakening of the body and a resurrection of a spiritual body capable and fitted for eternal life" (p. 39).
- "[House not made with hands] comprehends the eternal dwelling place of God, and the resurrected and glorified body of the redeemed in the life beyond the grave" (p. 45).
- "This collection of metaphors is a part of the Scripture reading of the Third Degree, and forms an appropriate introduction to the sublime ceremonies whose object is to teach symbolically the resurrection and life eternal" (p. 58).
- ". . . the very philosophy of Masonry teaches us that there can be no death without a resurrection, no decay without a subsequent restoration, no loss without eventual recovery" (p. 49).

These teachings are quite surprising from an organization that claims it is just a fraternity. Consider yet another comparison of the Lodge's teaching on resurrection with the teaching of the Church, noting the similarities and the one obvious difference. The Masonic Bible says that after a man's life has ended, "his soul returns to God who gave it and his body which returns to dust shall be raised, incorruptible and glorified and qualified for entrance into the Grand Lodge of the Celestial City of God" (p. 11). The Church says this:

> In death, the separation of the soul from the body, the human body decays and the soul goes to meet God, while awaiting its reunion with its glorified body. God, in his almighty power, will definitively grant incorruptible life to

our bodies by reuniting them with our souls, through the power of Jesus' Resurrection. (CCC 997)

While both the Lodge and the Church teach that our bodies will be raised incorruptible and glorified to everlasting life, the Church teaches that this will be accomplished through the power of Jesus' resurrection. Just how our mortal bodies will rise to life after death exceeds our imagination and understanding. The Church teaches that this truth is accessible only to faith (cf. CCC 1000). But in Freemasonry, this faith is not based on a belief in Jesus Christ. It was the problem of Masonry's teaching on the resurrection that finally convinced me to the leave the Lodge. Although I was not yet conversant with the Church's teaching on indifferentism, for me it came down to a simple formula:

(A) Freemasonry believes in a bodily resurrection to the celestial lodge above +

(B) Freemasonry does not believe in the necessity of faith in Jesus Christ =
Freemasonry is incompatible with Christianity.

Christian Masons often defend the Lodge's teachings by arguing that all people have a general hope of eternal life, and Freemasonry is only encouraging that hope. The Church would agree that it is commonly accepted among peoples that life continues in a spiritual fashion after death (cf. CCC 996). But the Lodge's detailed doctrinal statements concerning bodily resurrection and immortality, coupled with the exemplification of the doctrines in the Hiramic Legend, go beyond a vague hope for life after death. In the Master Mason degree, immortality is presented as an unmistakable truth into which the candidate is initiated. Moreover, because not all religions believe in bodily resurrection proves that Masonry has its own religious beliefs, *independent* of the faith of its members.

Resurrection of the body is a supernatural truth that God has progressively revealed to his people over the course of salvation history (cf. CCC 992). But God's progressive revelation of the resurrection to humanity has been perfectly and completely fulfilled in the resurrection of Jesus Christ. In fact, Jesus links faith in the resurrection to his own person: "I am the resurrection and the life" (Jn 11:25). It is Jesus himself who on the last day will raise up those who have believed in him, who have eaten his body and drunk his blood (cf. Jn 6:54). "For this is the will of my Father, that every one who sees the Son and believes in him should have eternal life; and I will raise him up at the last day" (Jn 6:40). Also in St. John's Gospel, we read: "No one can come to me unless the Father who sent me draws him; and I will raise him up at the last day" (6:44). Without Jesus Christ, there is no resurrection from the dead. St. Paul says that "if Christ has not been raised, then our preaching is in vain and your faith is in vain.... If Christ has not been raised, your faith is futile and you are still in your sins" (1 Cor 15:14, 17). Jesus' resurrection is the crowning truth of Christian faith (cf. CCC 638).

Because Jesus Christ is the resurrection and the life, no new rituals, legends, or "revelations" can modify or complement the revelation fulfilled by Christ. "Christian faith cannot accept 'revelations' that claim to surpass or correct the Revelation of which Christ is the fulfillment, as is the case in certain non-Christian religions and also in certain recent sects which base themselves on such 'revelations' " (CCC 67). We await no further new public revelation until the Lord Jesus comes again in glory (cf. 1 Tim 6:14; Titus 2:13).[71]

By omitting Jesus Christ from its teachings on the resurrection, the Lodge demonstrates that Christ is not essential to its doctrine. One does not have to believe in Jesus to be a Mason.

---

[71] Second Vatican Council, *Dei Verbum*, No. 4.

This distorts the truth of the resurrection and turns it into a lie (cf. Rom 1:25). While Masonic ritual does not make any doctrinal statements about Jesus, it deliberately ignores him. The Church condemns as heretical this and any other teaching about bodily resurrection without a concomitant affirmation of the supreme majesty of Jesus Christ, who is the resurrection and the life.

Asserting that Christ is the only source of mankind's salvation does not mean, however, that only Christians will be saved. The Church has always taught that "those who, through no fault of their own, do not know the gospel of Christ or his Church, but who nevertheless seek God with a sincere heart, and, moved by grace, try in their actions to do his will as they know it through the dictates of their conscience — those too may achieve eternal salvation."[72] According to Blessed Pius IX, such people could be saved because they are guilty only of "invincible ignorance."[73] But, again, this does not lessen the Church's obligation and sacred right to evangelize all men, particularly those who are in a spiritually deficient condition (cf. CCC 848). Since salvation for all is the will of God and salvation is founded upon the truth (cf. CCC 851), the errors of the Lodge compel all Christians to bear witness to the truth of Jesus Christ, out of love for God and for the truth.

Christians thus proclaim that Jesus Christ has completed the revelation of the resurrection and will raise us up on the last day. In fact, in a certain way, Christians have already risen with Christ (cf. CCC 1002). While the Lodge claims the Hiramic Legend raises the Mason to the faith of salvation, the Christian, by virtue of the Holy Spirit, has been participating in the death and resurrection of Christ from the moment of his baptism (cf. CCC 1002). "And you were buried with him in baptism, in which you

---

[72] Second Vatican Council, *Lumen Gentium*, No. 16.
[73] Encyclical, *Quanto Conficiamur Moerore* (August 10, 1863), No. 7.

were also raised with him through faith in the working of God, who raised him from the dead. . . . If then you have been raised with Christ, seek the things that are above, where Christ is, seated at the right hand of God" (Col 2:12; 3:1). "What is essentially new about Christian death is this: through Baptism, the Christian has already 'died with Christ' sacramentally, in order to live a new life; and if we die in Christ's grace, physical death completes this 'dying with Christ' and so completes our incorporation into him in his redeeming act" (CCC 1010).

In addition to the explicit teachings on resurrection, Masonry teaches about what happens to our souls after death:

> The Masonic idea of death . . . is represented only as a physical sleep for an unknown period of time, from which there will be an awakening of the body and a resurrection of a spiritual body capable and fitted for eternal life. From beginning to end the rituals of Freemasonry teach and symbolize the doctrine of man's immortality and repudiate every iota of the doctrine of annihilation at death. (Masonic Bible, p. 39)

This teaching of the soul's physically sleeping for an unknown period of time is not a Catholic belief. "Soul sleep" is a doctrine held by other religions, such as Seventh-day Adventists. Unlike the Lodge, the Church does not teach that the soul goes into hibernation after death. Instead, the soul is subject to judgment at the very moment of death, with immediate reward or punishment. "The New Testament speaks of judgment primarily in its aspect of the final encounter with Christ in his second coming, but also repeatedly affirms that each will be rewarded immediately after death in accordance with his works and faith" (CCC 1021). The resurrection of the dead, which will reunite our bodies and souls, will precede the Last Judgment (cf. CCC 1038), "the hour . . . when all who are in the tombs will hear [the Son of man's] voice and come forth, those who have done good, to the resurrection of life, and those who have done evil, to the resurrection of judgment" (Jn 5:28-29).

Freemasonry's doctrine on the resurrection and the immortality of the soul also lacks any specific catechesis of the eternal reality of judgment and hell. "The teaching of the Church affirms the existence of hell and its eternity. Immediately after death the souls of those who die in a state of mortal sin descend into hell, where they suffer the punishments of hell, 'eternal fire' " (CCC 1035). Masonry's omission of the reality of hell from its teachings on good works, immortality, and resurrection to the glorious lodge above is really a sin against hope, namely that of presumption (cf. CCC 2091). The Mason is taught to presume upon his own capacities to save himself. The Mason may also presume upon God's almighty power and mercy, hoping to obtain forgiveness without conversion (cf. CCC 2092). In such situations, man cannot fully respond to God's divine love. Hope is not only the confident expectation of divine blessing and the beatific vision of God; it is also the fear of offending God's love and of incurring punishment (cf. CCC 2090). Freemasonry says nothing about God's love for mankind, nor how men are obligated to respond to God's love with love. As St. Paul says, without this love for God, we are nothing (1 Cor 13:2).

Most contemporary Masons, whether Christian or non-Christian, are uncomfortable with the Masonic teaching of bodily resurrection. Those who contend that Freemasonry is just a fraternity have a considerable problem proving their case in the face of these religious teachings. Some Masons, accordingly, attempt to deny the Lodge's teachings on resurrection. They point out that Hiram was only reinterred, not raised from the dead. They argue this point because the lecture following the degree provides that "Hiram Abif was three times buried: first, in the rubbish of the

Temple; second, on the brow of a hill West of Mount Moriah; and third and lastly, as near the unfinished Sanctum Sanctorum, or Holy of Holies, as the Jewish Law would permit."[74]

The problem with this argument is that the ritual and a plethora of other Masonic authorities expressly state that the raising of the candidate symbolically testifies to the Masonic faith in the resurrection of the body. While the Masonic lecture provides that Hiram was *literally* reburied, it also shows him being *symbolically* raised from the dead. Masons making the reinterment argument do not only fail to accept the plain meaning of their rituals; they also forget that Freemasonry is "veiled in allegory which will unfold its beauties to the candid and industrious inquirer."[75] In the words of Joseph Fort Newton, "How many Masons fail to grasp the master truth of the Master Degree!"[76]

Another problem with the reinterment argument is that the candidate is never reburied, either actually or symbolically, at any time after the raising. After the prayer for salvation, the candidate is raised from the grave and is immediately caused to communicate with the Worshipful Master (through the exchange of the Grand Masonic Word). If Hiram were dead, one wonders how he could communicate with King Solomon.

In the allegorical drama, the Masonic prayer for salvation given at the grave has been answered. Hiram is alive again. He has been raised to the celestial lodge above. If not, then Masonry's most sublime degree would be nothing more than an exemplification of a murder and funeral. What would be the point?

The second argument Masons pose is that Hiram Abif could not have been raised from the dead because the ritual says that he was "in a high state of putrefaction," with his "flesh cleaving from

[74] Wisconsin Multiple Letter Cipher, 138.
[75] Ibid., 58.
[76] *The Builders, A Story and Study of Freemasonry*, 270-271.

the bone." But the fact that our bodies decay after death is the very essence of the mystery of the resurrection! "What is sown is perishable, what is raised is imperishable" (1 Cor 15:42). If decomposition could prevent the resurrection of the body, then none of us — except a few incorrupt saints — would, as Jesus promised, be "raised on the last day" (cf. Jn 6:40, 44, 54).

Those Christian Masons who do acknowledge the teachings of the Lodge can only resort to claiming that they view the resurrection of Hiram Abif in the context of their Christian faith. Yet the Hiramic Legend is not presented within the framework of a Christian worldview. While the object of Masonry's third degree is to demonstrate the reality of life after death, the Lodge, consistent with its other teachings, makes no reference to the reality of sin, which cannot be disconnected from death. All men have been implicated in Adam's sin, (cf. CCC 402), and death is a consequence of this sin (cf. CCC 1008). "Sin came into the world through one man and death through sin, and so death spread to all men because all men sinned" (Rom 5:12). Of course, if Masonry can ignore sin, it can also ignore Jesus Christ, "the Lamb of God, who takes away the sin of the world" (Jn 1:29).

Though the curse of sin and death is universal, salvation from sin and death in Jesus Christ is also universal. "Then as one man's trespass led to condemnation for all men, so one man's act of righteousness leads to acquittal and life for all men" (Rom 5:18). For the Christian, this death resulting from sin is transformed, not by imitating the conduct of Hiram Abif, but by the propitiatory sacrifice of Jesus Christ, the Son of God, who changed the curse of death into a blessing (cf. CCC 1009). By his Passover, Christ opened to all men the fountain of baptism and thus the kingdom of God (cf. CCC 1225). Only the light of divine revelation, which the Lodge rejects, clarifies the reality of sin, which continues to weigh heavily on human life and history (cf. CCC 386-87). Without revelation, we cannot recognize sin clearly; nor can we grasp the meaning of salvation history, which is revealed only in the light of the death and resurrection of Jesus Christ (cf. CCC 388).

Hence, with an insufficient understanding of the reality of sin, the Lodge teaches the Mason that he is responsible for his own salvation. Hiram Abif is presented as the exemplar of how a Mason is to save himself through his own efforts:

> Masonry teaches that redemption and salvation are both the power and the responsibility of the individual Mason. Saviors like Hiram Abiff can and do show the way, but men must always follow and demonstrate, each for himself, his power to save himself, to build his own spiritual fabric in his own time and way. Every man in essence is his own savior and redeemer; for if he does not save himself, he will not be saved.[77]

Freemasonry's death-and-resurrection rite of the third degree is taken, not from sacred revelation, but from the ancient mystery religions. The parallels between the Legend of the Third Degree of Masonry and the ancient mystery religions are noteworthy. Dr. Ronald H. Nash, a Protestant professor of philosophy at Reformed Theological Seminary, Orlando, has identified five basic traits common in mystery religions:[78]

1. The use of symbolism to represent the natural processes of growth, death, decay, and rebirth.
2. The use of secret ceremonies, often in connection with an initiation rite. Mystery religions also passed on a "secret" to

---

[77] Lynn F. Perkins, *The Meaning of Masonry*, 95.

[78] "Was the New Testament Influenced by Pagan Religions?" *Christian Research Journal* (Winter 1994). Various Grand Lodges have also confirmed Masonry's connection to the pagan mystery religions (e.g., Texas, *The Holy Bible* [October 2001]; Nevada, *Masonic Monitor* [November 1972]).

the initiates, whereby they might achieve unity with the deity.

3. A central myth in which a character either returns to life after death or else triumphs over his enemies. Implicit in the myth is the theme of redemption from everything earthly and temporal.

4. Concern for the emotional life of followers rather than commitment to correct belief. This de-emphasis on correct belief marks an important difference between the mysteries and Christianity. The Christian faith recognizes only one legitimate path to God, Jesus Christ. The mysteries, on the other hand, were inclusivistic. Nothing prevented a believer in one cult from following other mysteries as well.

5. Mystical experience of union with their God as the immediate goal of the initiates.

To evaluate the story of Hiram Abif in light of both Christianity and the ancient mystery religions, let us examine the parallels:

1. In the mystery religions, the characters did not die for someone else. The notion of the Son of God dying in place of his creatures is unique to Christianity. Hiram Abif died for no one else.

2. In the mystery religions, the characters do not die for the sins of the world. Only Jesus died for sin. Hiram dies for virtue and honor because he will not disclose esoteric Masonic knowledge.

3. In the mystery religions, the gods go through repeated deaths and resuscitations, symbolizing nature's annual cycle. Jesus died only once. His sacrifice on Calvary is eternally present in the Holy Sacrifice of the Mass.

4. In the mystery religions, the death of the mystical character has no historical basis. Jesus' death, however, was an actual event in history. The legend of Hiram Abif has no historical basis.

5. In the mystery religions, the characters do not die voluntarily. Hiram Abif tried to avoid death. Our Lord was not taken by the "Grim Tyrant Death," as it is called in Masonry's third degree. Rather, he offered himself as a volitional sacrifice for the sins of the world.

In each of the above instances, Hiram Abif's story bears a close resemblance to the ancient mystery religions. Masonry's symbolic use of the setting maul, spade, coffin, scythe, and sprig of acacia in the Hiramic Legend also resembles the vegetation theme of death, decay, and rebirth seen in ancient mystery religions. Further, the religious faith of Freemasonry, like that of Christianity, culminates in the proclamation of the resurrection of the body. But unlike the Lodge, Christianity firmly proclaims, believes, and hopes that, just as Christ is truly risen from the dead and lives forever, so after death the righteous will live forever with the risen Christ. Paul tells us this: "If the Spirit of him who raised Jesus from the dead dwells in you, he who raised Christ Jesus from the dead will give life to your mortal bodies also through his Spirit who dwells in you" (Rom 8:11; cf. 1 Cor 6:14, 2 Cor 4:14, Phil 3:10-11, 1 Thess 4:14).

Burial Rites

To this point, the Lodge's doctrines and practices that we have examined have been limited to what is taught in the secrecy of the lodge room. However, Freemasonry has very formal religious burial rites for its members that it celebrates publicly. The Masonic

Bible explains: "From time immemorial religious cults ... have given special attention to the burial of their dead, and solemn rituals have been used in the last rites of fellow members. Masons are no exception to this matter" (p. 35). These services provide an opportunity for non-Masons to learn about the religious teachings of the Lodge. At these burial services, the public can also see Freemasons in Masonic attire, wearing their aprons and white gloves.

These services are usually conducted by the members of the deceased Mason's lodge and take place at a funeral home or in the family's church or place of worship. The Worshipful Master or a designated Mason makes the presentation. Henry Coil explains that the purpose of the Masonic memorial service is "to commit the body of a deceased brother to the dust whence it came and to speed the liberated spirit back to the Great Source of Light." Coil adds that "[m]any Freemasons make this flight with no other guarantee of a safe landing than their belief in the religion of Freemasonry."[79]

Masonic memorial services for deceased Masons are common throughout the United States. Typically, they include a formal address to the family, followed by Masonic prayers and a ceremonial depositing of the Masonic apron and sprig of acacia in the coffin. These services are not intended to interfere with any other religious services the family has requested.

Typical of the oration made by a representative of the Lodge at the opening of a Masonic memorial service is the assurance that death is not the ultimate sleep but a glorious awakening. The spokesman assures grieving family and friends that their loved one has been "raised from silent death to a glorious life eternal."[80] The

---

[79] *Coil's Masonic Encyclopedia*, 512.
[80] Wisconsin Masonic Handbook, *Ceremonies*, X-72 (1999).

service includes specific prayers whose purpose is to comfort the mourners with the news that the deceased, having been faithful to his Masonic duties, now dwells in the celestial lodge above, where his soul has been "translated from the imperfections of this mortal sphere to that all-perfect and glorious home where God, the Grand Architect of the Universe, presides."[81] These religious doctrines of resurrection and union with God are preached, of course, without acknowledging any need whatever for Christ the Savior.

At the conclusion of Masonic memorial services, the Worshipful Master deposits the decedent's Masonic apron in the casket (or places the apron next to the remains if his body has been cremated). This is the apron the Mason received right after being symbolically raised to eternal life in the Master Mason degree. (In many cases, the decedent is already clothed with his apron, so depositing it is unnecessary.) The Worshipful Master explains to the deceased Mason's family and friends that the Masonic apron is a reminder of the "purity of life that is necessary to gain admission to the celestial lodge."[82]

Attendant to the depositing of the apron is the depositing of the sprig of acacia. As we have seen, the sprig of acacia facilitated the discovery of Hiram's body in the third degree. Masons in attendance gather in a single-file line, approach the decedent's casket, and place a sprig of acacia on his chest (or by the urn). Because Hiram Abif was later raised to eternal life, the spokesman explains that the "evergreen is an emblem of our faith in the immortality of the soul."[83] If the service includes seeing the deceased Mason to the gravesite, Masons may gather in what they call "the Mystic Chain" around the grave:

---

[81] Ibid., X-74.
[82] Ibid., X-138.
[83] Ibid., X-74.

This is the formation of the Brethren in a circle, holding each other by the hands. Each brother crosses his arms in front of his body, giving his right hand to his left hand neighbor and his left hand to his right hand neighbor. It is a symbol of the close connection of all Masons in a common brotherhood, and is usually practiced around the grave in Masonic Burials. (Masonic Bible, p. 25)

Masonic memorial services give the public a good idea about the religious teachings of Freemasonry. While the Masonic memorial service may give the deceased Mason's family comfort during a time of grieving, the Lodge's teachings on the decedent's eternal security in the celestial lodge without any mention of Christ are repugnant to the Christian faith and the perennial teachings of the Church.

Chapter

V

MASONIC SECRECY AND DECEPTION

Having studied the primary doctrines and practices of the Lodge, let us turn now to how Freemasonry attracts and keeps its members.

Recruitment

Men are generally introduced to Freemasonry by family members or close friends. Candidates are told very little about the inner workings of Freemasonry, and nothing about its religious teachings. As a result, most candidates base their decision to join Freemasonry on the relationship they have with a Masonic friend or relative. Because their information comes almost exclusively from men they trust, candidates automatically have a favorable perception of the organization. Almost never do candidates independently research Freemasonry; there seems to be no need. Their knowledge of the Lodge typically does not go beyond its fancy Masonic rings, lapel pins, and bumper stickers. If a candidate comes upon negative information about Masonry, he usually decides to trust his Masonic friend rather than a source he does not personally know.

In introducing candidates to Masonry, Masons describe the organization as the most ancient and honorable fraternity in the world. They emphasize the exclusive nature of the organization. Allusions to the esoteric and secret nature of Freemasonry pique a man's curiosity and enhance the Lodge's mystique. Candidates are informed that they must be unanimously accepted into the fraternity. They may even be told of men who have been black-balled by a lodge, though rejection of a candidate is extremely rare. This is done to heighten the perceived privilege of membership. Masons also explain to nonmembers that Freemasonry provides many advantages, particularly in the business world, as well as a social support system for wives and children. The brethren, the candidate is assured, "take care of their own."

Candidates are given pamphlets that provide appealing information about Freemasonry. These invariably include a list of the famous men of Freemasonry, the various charitable activities of the organization, and all of the wonderful social events the fraternity holds for Masons and their wives. Some lodges invite candidates and their families to a "Friends Night" social at the Masonic temple. At these events, a film about Masonic charity and fraternity is shown, followed by warm fellowship in the lodge's dining hall. Candidates experience the aura of the Lodge. Masonry appears to be a secret organization of society's elite, dedicated to improving a man's self-worth and the community at large.

In spite of all of these efforts at recruitment, Freemasonry claims that candidates are not solicited to join the Lodge. Future members must *ask* for the privilege of becoming Masons. A famous Masonic slogan is "Ask 1 to Be 1." Nevertheless, most candidates are, in fact, directly or indirectly solicited to join Freemasonry. Many are simply asked to join or given a petition by a family member or best friend. If a father is a Mason, a son is expected to follow him. The success or failure of business relationships may hinge upon Masonic affiliation. There can be tremendous pressure to join Freemasonry. Concerned that Masonry's membership has consistently declined over the past twenty years, some Grand Lodges offer financial incentives to lodges that recruit new members.

A candidate for the Masonic degrees is given a document, furnished by the lodge, representing the man's formal request to join Freemasonry. After completing and signing his petition, he gives it to his sponsor, who, along with a second sponsoring member, adds his signature and sends the petition to the lodge. The petition must be read aloud in open lodge, typically at three consecutive regularly scheduled meetings. This may take two to six weeks. The petition identifies the applicant by his name, address, age, marital status, occupation, and religious affiliation. In it, the applicant declares his desire to be initiated into the mysteries of Freemasonry.

During these few weeks, the candidate is interviewed, usually three different times, by three different members of the lodge he has petitioned. He may also be required to present himself for a group interview conducted by a committee of lodge members. During these interviews, the applicant is repeatedly told that a Mason must believe in God, but that religion is never to be discussed in the lodge room, thus beginning a process of desensitization. If, after these assurances, the candidate hears prayers offered up to the GAOTU and partakes in solemn religious rituals, the candidate would think back to these representations and hopefully conclude that "God is not being discussed in the lodge."

Catholics are special targets for the desensitization process. The Lodge seems to make special efforts to achieve a healthy Catholic representation in its ranks. Catholic candidates are told that the Church has a favorable impression of the Lodge. They are assured that any misgivings the Church has had in the past were directed toward European Masonry, and that even this sentiment has eroded. Freemasons attempt to prove their point by claiming that the previous penalty of excommunication for Catholic membership in the Lodge has been abrogated (this is not true and is discussed in Chapter VII). Catholics are even told that the Pope's highest cardinals are Masons and that one must be a Mason in order to be eligible for entry into the Swiss Guards (the papal "secret service").

During the interview process, the candidate is asked whether his wife or any family members know about Freemasonry. The candidate is pressed to disclose what his relatives know, how they know it, and whether they have any objections to his joining the organization. Many interviewers request that a candidate's wife be present. Freemasonry wants to make sure that there will be no restrictions on a man's dedication to the organization, or any pressure from outside parties that could negatively influence his Masonic affiliation.

After the interview process is completed and the petition is read for the third time in lodge, the members vote by secret ballot to accept or reject the candidate. White cubes signify acceptance; black balls, rejections. A unanimous vote is required. After the election, the successful candidate is informed that he has been unanimously accepted into the fraternity. This process, perhaps accompanied by calls from Masonic family and friends, makes the candidate feel special and leads to the much anticipated evening on which the first Masonic degree is conferred.

Events leading up to the conferral of the first degree, therefore, give a candidate a positive perception of American Freemasonry. The candidate is not given any reason to investigate Freemasonry further, and unfortunately, most men do not. An educated Christian informed in advance about Masonry's religious teachings — especially the death-and-resurrection rite that never mentions

Christ — may well have second thoughts about his involvement
with the Lodge.

Initiation

On the evening of the long-awaited first degree, the candidate
arrives at the lodge at the specified time and is greeted by the
brethren. After brief introductions, the candidate waits in the ante-
room. The lodge is ceremonially opened and the Junior and Senior
Deacons come out to where the candidate is anxiously waiting.
"Do you solemnly declare, upon your honor," the Senior Deacon
asks the candidate, "that, unbiased by friends and uninfluenced
by mercenary motives, you freely and voluntarily offer yourself a
candidate for the mysteries of Freemasonry?"[1]

This requirement appears odd because most candidates are
indeed influenced to join Freemasonry because of the bias of their
Masonic friends. Prospective members are also solicited to join
Freemasonry on the basis of potential advantages in the business
world. Yet, the candidate is now asked by the Lodge to promise
that he is not joining Masonry for these reasons.

After the candidate so promises, the Junior Deacon explains
to him that "Masonry consists of a course in ancient hieroglyph-
ical and moral instruction, taught according to ancient usage by
types, emblems and allegorical figures." The candidate is told to
lay aside all thought of levity and address his mind to the solemn
truths he is about to learn. He is then assured that nothing will be
required of him that does not tend toward his own good or the
usefulness of his fellow men.[2]

Without additional explanation, the candidate is told to strip
down to his underwear. He is then given a special Masonic gar-

---

[1] Kentucky Monitor, 4.
[2] Wisconsin Multiple Letter Cipher, 34.

ment and slippers. This requirement to remove one's clothing surprises most candidates. But since they believe Freemasonry is just a fraternity, the requirement seems harmless. The candidate, however, is also required to remove all jewelry, including wedding ring, crucifix, scapular, and other sacramentals so that he might "carry nothing offensive or defensive into the lodge."[3]

The discerning Christian should see a problem with this requirement. While Masons claim that Freemasonry encourages a man to practice his own faith, the institution requires the candidate to divest himself of all his religious reminders so as not to offend anyone or spiritually defend himself. The concepts of encouraging a man's faith and taking away the reminders of his faith are at odds. Nevertheless, under the pressure of the moment, with family and friends waiting inside the lodge room, most candidates comply. The candidate is then blindfolded, and a noose is placed around his neck, which the Lodge calls a "cabletow." "Symbolically," says Claudy, "the cabletow is the cord by which the Masonic infant is attached to his Mother Lodge."[4] The cabletow is also used to drag a candidate who refuses the ceremony out of the lodge.[5]

The candidate is virtually helpless. Nearly naked, divested of all jewelry and sacramentals, he has been blindfolded and secured by a rope around his neck. In this state of vulnerability, the candidate is properly prepared to receive the solemn truths of Freemasonry.

Now the candidate is led to the Inner Door (the entrance used by lodge initiates), on which he is to knock three times. The Senior Deacon then opens the door and asks, "Who comes here?" The

---

[3] Ibid., 47.
[4] Carl H. Claudy, *Introduction to Freemasonry*, Vol. 1, *Entered Apprentice*, 40.
[5] Wisconsin Multiple Letter Cipher, 48.

Junior Deacon responds for the candidate: "Mr. ————, who has long been in darkness, and now seeks to be brought to light, and to receive a part in the rights and benefits of this worshipful lodge, erected to God and dedicated to the Holy Saints John, as all brothers and fellows have done before." The Senior Deacon then demands of the candidate, "Is this an act of your own free will and accord?" After the candidate affirms that it is, the Senior Deacon asks the Junior Deacon whether the candidate "is worthy and well-qualified, duly and truly prepared."[6] That being affirmed, the Senior Deacon asks whether the candidate is "of lawful age and properly vouched for."[7] After another affirmation, the Senior Deacon asks by what further right the candidate expects to obtain such an important privilege. The Junior Deacon responds, "By being a man, free-born, of good report, and well-recommended."[8] The Senior Deacon closes the door and provides the favorable report to the Worshipful Master.

The candidate has only a few seconds to reflect upon this exchange. Though he has been blindfolded for only a couple of minutes, the Junior Deacon has just declared that he has "long been in darkness." Freemasonry is clear that the candidate's darkness relates, not just to his ignorance of a few fraternity passwords, *but to his customary spiritual condition*:

> In Freemasonry . . . darkness is a symbol of ignorance; while light is the symbol of enlightenment and knowledge. It is a principle of Freemasonry that the natural eye cannot perceive of the mysteries of the Order until the heart has embraced the deep spiritual and mystic meanings of those sublime mysteries. Hence, all applicants for the Degrees of

---

[6] Ibid., 35.
[7] Ibid.
[8] Ibid.

Freemasonry are required to enter the Lodge in total darkness, this darkness is preparatory and preliminary to his receiving the light he desires and searches. (Masonic Bible, p. 39)

It should be offensive to any Christian to be declared to be in such a state of spiritual darkness. By virtue of baptism, all Christians have been freed from the power of darkness and made children of God (cf. CCC 1250). Through Christ, God has called them out of darkness and into his marvelous light (cf. 1 Pet 2:9). "I have come as light into the world," says the Lord, "that whoever believes in me may not remain in darkness" (Jn 12:46).

The Church uses the term *rebirth* to describe the sacraments that give us new life in Christ through whom we have become children of God (cf. CCC 1692). But while the Christian's rebirth is brought about by water and the Spirit (cf. Jn 3:5), the Mason's rebirth is symbolically achieved by his initiation into the Lodge. Allen Roberts, in his popular book on Freemasonry, has this to say to the candidate: "Your preparation for your entrance into Freemasonry began the day your mother brought you into the world. Your entrance into the lodge for initiation became, symbolically, your rebirth."[9] Albert Mackey elaborates on the spiritual, moral, and intellectual condition of the candidate as he waits outside the lodge room:

Having been wandering amid the errors and covered over with the pollutions of the outer and profane world, he comes inquiringly to our doors, seeking the new birth, and asking a withdrawal of the veil which conceals divine truth from his uninitiated sight. . . . There is to be, not simply a change for the future, but also an extinction of the past . . . the

---

[9] *The Craft and Its Symbols*, 13.

chains of error and ignorance which have previously restrained the candidate in moral and intellectual captivity are broken.[10]

The Lodge thus views the Christian, who has been reborn into the death and resurrection of Jesus Christ, as being in a spiritually deficient condition. He must die to his former life in Christ and be reborn into the new life of the Lodge. Before the candidate has sufficient time for reflection, the Senior Deacon ushers the candidate into the lodge room for the first time. After taking a few steps, the candidate is received by the Senior Deacon on the point of a sharp instrument piercing his naked left breast. "As this is an instrument of torture to your flesh," the Senior Deacon intones, "so should the recollection of it be to your conscience should you ever presume to reveal the secrets of Freemasonry unlawfully."[11]

The blindfolded candidate is then conducted to the center of the lodge and made to kneel. He is required to profess a belief in deity. If the candidate professes a belief in any deity whatsoever, he is told that his faith is well founded. He is then caused to rise and continue his Masonic journey around the lodge room, escorted by the Senior Deacon, as a psalm is recited. This procedure of walking the blindfolded candidate around the lodge room is called "circumambulation" and reminds us of Jesus' words: "Walk while you have the light, lest the darkness overtake you; he who walks in the darkness does not know where he goes" (Jn 12:35).

The candidate is stopped three times — at the stations of the Junior Warden, Senior Warden, and Worshipful Master. As before, each officer asks the candidate if his participation is of his own free will and accord. Since the candidate does not really know what will be further required of him, the question is unfair. Invariably he

---

[10] *Masonic Ritualist*, 23.
[11] Wisconsin Multiple Letter Cipher, 36.

answers yes. These repeated inquiries, which require the apprehensive candidate to affirm in front of the brothers that his participation is voluntary, condition him to accept what he is experiencing.

After the candidate passes the examination by the officers, the Worshipful Master directs the Senior Deacon to escort him back "to the West" — one step directly behind the altar. The Worshipful Master then instructs the Senior Deacon to teach the candidate to approach the East by "one regular upright step, his feet forming the angle of an oblong square, his body erect before the Worshipful Master in the East."[12] The Senior Deacon instructs the candidate to take one step with his left foot and bring the heel of the right foot to the hollow of the left. This done, the Senior Deacon informs the Worshipful Master that the candidate is "in order."

As the candidate stands blindfolded before the altar, the Worshipful Master informs him that he is required to swear a solemn and binding oath. "It is one we have all taken before you," he tells the candidate, adding the assurance that there is nothing contained in the obligation that would conflict with any duty the candidate owes to God, country, neighbor, or himself. This assurance can hardly be genuine when the Worshipful Master has no idea about the candidate's religious beliefs (which is generally the case). The Worshipful Master then asks whether the candidate wishes to proceed. Again, under the pressure of the moment, most candidates consent.

The candidate is asked to kneel at the Masonic altar in a particular way and place his hands in a particular position on the Holy Bible (or whatever book he deems sacred), left hand underneath and right hand over the top of the book. The Senior Deacon then declares to the Worshipful Master that the candidate is in "due form." At this point, the Worshipful Master raps three

---

[12] Wisconsin Multiple Letter Cipher, 39.

times, descends the dais, and approaches the altar. The brothers not participating in the degree leave their seats on the sidelines, form two parallel lines between the altar and the East, and face each other. All lights are turned off. The candidate is then instructed to swear the oath of the degree by repeating the words of the Worshipful Master.

Covenant Oaths

For each of the three Masonic degrees, the required oath is similar. Essentially the same throughout the world, these oaths require a man to preserve and protect Masonry's hidden mysteries, keep secret its passwords and handshakes, uphold its laws and regulations, and maintain partiality and charity among brother Masons and their relatives, thereby "faithfully conforming his life to the teachings of the Order" (Masonic Bible, p. 52).

Most men who obligate themselves to Freemasonry by these oaths do not understand the concomitant moral problems. This is understandable; most Masons are not familiar with moral theology. The Masonic Bible (p. 52) gives a fair statement of the nature of an oath as "a solemn attestation before God of the truth of the declarations being made, involving the punishment of his just wrath in the event of untruthfulness or as a consequence of its violation." An oath is much graver than the promises or pledges that are often required by fraternities because it asks God to intervene, both in witnessing the statement and assisting in the fulfillment of its promises. Because it formally invokes God's participation, an oath subjects the oath-taker to divine judgment and, in Masonry's case, a conditional self-curse (through the penalties discussed later).

For example, the beginning of each Masonic oath commences with these words: "In the presence of Almighty God, and this Worshipful Lodge . . . I most solemnly and sincerely promise and swear." As these words are said, the Worshipful Master, who administers the oath, presses down on the candidate's hands, which rest upon the Bible, to impress upon him the sacred nature of the oath. Further, the end of each oath concludes with this typical execratory formula: "All this I most solemnly and sincerely promise and swear . . . so help me God, and keep me steadfast in the due performance of the same."

Fraternal pledges, by contrast, do not formally call on God to assist in keeping the promise (otherwise they are not pledges; they are oaths). As such, fraternal pledges do not use formulas such as "So help me God" or "I solemnly swear before Almighty God." Instead, the pledge-giver invokes his own name in making the promise: "I give you my word."

Such pledges are thus given upon the honor and reputation of the person making the promise. Consequently, the pledge-giver is to be judged on his own word and does not expressly place himself under God's judgment. As to those men who would rather give an affirmation than swear an oath to God, the Masonic Bible (p. 24) says, "Affirmations instead of oaths are entirely inadmissible in Freemasonry."

Unlike Masonic oaths, fraternal pledges are usually read to the individual before he is asked to make his promise. This is done so that the candidate may fully realize what he is promising. This happens in the pledge of secrecy given by the Knights of Columbus. In Freemasonry, the oaths are not read to the candidate in advance. The candidate is simply assured that the oath will not conflict with any duty he owes to God, his country, his neighbor, or himself, and he is asked to repeat the words of the Worshipful Master.

The Masonic oath is also distinguishable from licit oaths because it is sworn in secret. For example, by means of a public oath one enters into marriage; lawyers promise to uphold the Constitution; and a witness promises to tell the truth about serious matters before a court. While fraternal pledges are usually done in secret, licit oaths are done publicly. If the subject matter is serious and beneficial to the community, what is there to hide?

It is the Masonic oath, or "obligation," that makes a man a Freemason. When the candidate assumes this obligation, he solemnly binds himself to Freemasonry and takes on certain duties that are his for the rest of his life. Throughout the ceremonies of opening and closing every lodge meeting, the Worshipful Master twice asks the Senior Warden, "What makes you a Mason?" The Senior Warden answers, "My obligation."

The candidate makes various promises of self-donation to Freemasonry and to his brothers, binding himself by oath and under penalty of grisly death. Penalties for the Entered Apprentice, Fellowcraft, and Master Mason are, respectively, as follows:

> Of having my throat cut across, my tongue torn out, and with my body buried in the sands of the sea at low-water mark, where the tide ebbs and flows twice in twenty-four hours, should I ever knowingly or willfully violate this, my solemn Obligation of an Entered Apprentice. So help me God and make me steadfast to keep and perform the same. (Nevada Ritual, 19)

> Of having my left breast torn open, my heart plucked out and placed on the highest pinnacle of the temple, there to be devoured by the vultures of the air, should I ever knowingly violate this, my Fellow Craft obligation. So help me God and keep me steadfast in the due performance of the same. (Wisconsin Multiple Letter Cipher, 79)

> Of having my body severed in twain, my bowels taken thence and burned to ashes, the ashes scattered to the four winds of heaven, that no more remembrance might be had

of so vile a wretch as I should be to knowingly violate this, my Master Mason obligation. So help me God and keep me steadfast in the due performance of the same. (Wisconsin Multiple Letter Cipher, 114)

When a penalty, whether actual or symbolic, is attached to an oath, it is known as a self-curse.[13] "The obsecration of a Freemason," Mackey explains, "simply means that if he violates his vows or betrays his trust, he is worthy of such penalty, and that if such penalty were inflicted on him, it would be just and proper."[14] In essence, the Mason swears, "I'll be damned." Further, because the oath is sworn to God and not men, Mackey explains that the punishment of the self-curse is "to be inflicted by God, and not by men."[15] This is why Claudy describes the punishment as "the wrath of God blasphemed. The horror of a sin of which there is none greater."[16]

Masons cannot defend these oaths without putting themselves in the proverbial catch-22. Either the oaths mean what they say, or they do not. If they mean what they say, then the Mason is swearing that he would be worthy of the death penalty if he revealed trivial fraternal secrets or failed to live up to a code of moral conduct that was not explained to him in advance. If the oaths do not mean what they say, then the Mason is swearing profanities to God and liable to incurring his divine judgment.

---

[13] There is only one oath with a self-curse that is acceptable and pleasing to God. That is the oath he himself swore when he promised us salvation through the eternal sacrifice and everlasting priesthood of Jesus Christ (Ps 110:4; Heb 6:17-20). When God swore this oath on himself, he gave us his Word (Jn 1:14), and the Word became flesh and dwelled among us (Jn 1:14), and the Word took on the curse of our sins by being hung on a tree (Deut 21:23; Gal 3:13).

[14] *Mackey's Revised Encyclopedia of Freemasonry*, Vol. 2, 760.

[15] Ibid.

[16] Carl H. Claudy, *Foreign Countries: A Gateway to the Interpretation and Development of Certain Symbols of Freemasonry*, 90.

Many Masons attempt to defend the oaths by saying that they are not to be taken seriously. But this is one of the reasons the oath is immoral. Lest it be profane, an oath sworn to God must be taken seriously. When you consider the oath and the self-curse in the context of the lodge, where they are given by grown men, on the Bible, and at an altar in solemn religious ceremony, it is hard to understand how any Christian could not regard the oath seriously. For Masons to argue that their rituals are not to be taken seriously must also mean that the morality and godliness for which they strive cannot be taken seriously either.

Sacred Scripture is clear that taking oaths is a very serious matter before God. Jesus said, "Do not swear at all, either by heaven, for it is the throne of God, or by the earth, for it is his footstool, or by Jerusalem, for it is the city of the great King. And do not swear by your head, for you cannot make one hair white or black. Let what you say be simply 'Yes' or 'No'; anything more than this comes from evil" (Mt 5:34-37; cf. Jas 5:12). Jesus meant for Christians to be so truthful that people could believe them even without an oath. This does not mean Christians are forbidden to take oaths. Under certain conditions, an oath may be licit and an act of virtue. But its subject matter must be extremely serious (for example, in the sacrament of marriage or the proffering of legal testimony). The holiness of the divine name demands that we never use it for trivial matters (cf. CCC 2155). If the subject matter is trivial, the oath-taker uses the name of the Lord in vain (cf. CCC 2150).

No reasonable person would argue that preserving the pass-words *Boaz, Jachin,* and *Tubal-Cain* mandate a solemn oath invoking a self-curse and the Lord's judgment. I analogize this to a family who cherishes certain secret recipes that have been handed down to them from past generations. One can hardly imagine the father of the family summoning his children to the kitchen table, blindfolding them, and having them swear on the Bible that they would rather have their eyeballs pierced to the center with a three-inch blade, their feet flayed, and be forced to walk the hot sands of the sterile shores of the Red Sea until the flaming sun shall strike them with livid plague rather than give the recipe to someone outside the family. But that is the penalty of the oath the Christian swears on the Koran during his initiation into the Shriners!

The Second Commandment forbids these improper oaths and every improper use of God's name (cf. CCC 2150). Because God's name is sacred and unique, rejection of false oaths is a duty toward God (cf. CCC 2143; 2151). "As Creator and Lord, God is the norm of all truth. Human speech is either in accord with or in opposition to God who is Truth itself. When it is truthful and legitimate, an oath highlights the relationship of human speech with God's truth. A false oath calls on God to be witness to a lie" (CCC 2151).

The Mason may claim that the oath is not false or trivial because of the high moral standard the candidate is swearing to uphold. This does not explain why it is ever permissible for a Christian to swear to adhere to a code of conduct that has not been presented to him in advance. The Mason swears, among other things, that he will not have illicit sex with another Mason's wife, mother, sister, or daughter lest he be worthy of having his body cut in half. But our Lord has already condemned fornication and adultery. If the Church does not require such gruesome oaths, Freemasonry has no good reason to do so.

The Mason also swears, under the same penalty, that he will not cheat, wrong, or defraud a lodge of Master Masons or a brother Mason knowingly; nor will he strike a brother Master Mason except in self-defense. Since we are already bound by God's laws to love one another, including our enemies as ourselves, swearing such morbid oaths is an unnecessary and idle use of

God's name. In addition to the uselessness of these oaths, such declarations require the oath-taker to put his Masonic brothers and their relatives in a special class and give them preference over non-Masons. This conduct is immoral, even without an oath.

When pressed about the inappropriate subject matter of the oaths, Masons usually shift the discussion by saying that the penalties attached to the oaths are only symbolic. They usually don't say what the penalties are symbolic of, but this must necessarily be the torture and mutilation they symbolize unless the penalties, and hence the oaths, are just a sham. Their rebuttal also does not address why the oath is required in the first place; nor does it explain why the candidate swears to be subject to penalties that are never to be carried out. But even if the penalties are only symbolic, they are still not morally justified. No civil system of government would tolerate the murder or mutilation of one of its citizens for disclosing a password to a non-fraternity member. The penalty does not fit the crime. Moreover, the candidate is required to swear the oaths "without any hesitation, mental reservation, or secret evasion of mind whatever." It is hard to understand how such language assists the candidate in discerning what is symbolic and what is not.

Attaching these symbolic penalties to the oaths somehow suggests that the spiritual and moral obligations the Lodge imposes on its members are graver than those given to the faithful by the Church. But Christ did not impose on his disciples the requirement to swear oaths with self-curses. The Christian Mason might consider why such grotesque oaths were not required when he was baptized in the name of the Holy Trinity or sealed by the Holy Spirit in the sacrament of confirmation. He might also contemplate why those who are charged with the mission of bringing people to God do not declare these self-curses at their ordinations. A Christian would not expect to hear such blood-curdling profanity in the church parking lot, much less in the church itself.

That these graphic penalties are sworn on the Bible, even if they are only symbolic, shows a lack of respect for God and amount to blasphemy (cf. CCC 2149) which is a grave sin (cf. CCC 2148, 1369). They make the Christian swear that he would be worthy of defiling the temple of the Holy Spirit on the very Scriptures the Spirit inspired (cf. 1 Cor 6:19). Masons presumably have no intention of blaspheming the Lord's name when they take these oaths, but the Church teaches that blasphemy is always gravely illicit regardless of its surrounding circumstances and intentions (cf. CCC 1756, 1856).

Calling the penalties symbolic does not mean that they are not taken seriously. The Lodge constantly reminds its members of the symbolic penalties of the oaths they have taken. At various points in Masonic ritual and anytime a Mason addresses the Worshipful Master in open lodge, he must make two signs in reference to his Masonic oath, one after the other. The first, called the "Due Guard," refers to the positions in which his hands were placed on the Holy Bible (or other book he deemed sacred) while he swore the oath. The second, called "the Sign," is a gesture of self-mutilation that symbolizes the penalty of the Masonic oaths.

The Due Guard of an Entered Apprentice is displayed by simulating the left hand supporting the Holy Bible and the right hand resting thereon. The Due Guard of a Fellowcraft is displayed by pretending that the right hand is on the Bible while the left arm forms an upright square bent at ninety degrees. The Due Guard of a Master Mason is displayed by simulating both hands resting on the Bible. These Due Guards represent the position of the arms and hands during the oath and remind the Mason of the sacred nature of his obligation to Freemasonry.

The Entered Apprentice Sign refers to the slitting of the throat, which the Mason symbolizes by moving his right hand, palm down, across his throat from left to right. The Fellowcraft

Sign refers to tearing open the left breast to pluck out the heart. The Mason symbolizes this by moving the right hand formed like a claw over the chest, starting at the left breast and moving to the right. The Master Mason Sign refers to severing the body in two pieces to take out the bowels. The Mason symbolizes this by moving the right hand across the stomach, palm down, from left to right. These Signs, given at every regular Masonic assembly, remind the brethren of the binding nature of their oaths.

The bloody nature of the Masonic penalties also confirms the covenantal nature of the oaths. A contract is made by giving a promise, while a covenant is made only by swearing an oath. A covenant, therefore, is a sacred bond of interpersonal communion ("I am yours and you are mine").[17] Those baptized in Christ should be familiar with the term *covenant*. By becoming incarnate and giving his life for our sins, Jesus has established the new and everlasting covenant in his blood, uniting humanity to God through his beloved bride, the Church (cf. CCC 1612, 1621).

The "Masonic Covenant" is sealed with the blood-curdling penalty of the oath (cf. Masonic Bible, p. 38). Blood, whether actual or symbolic, has always been considered that which ratifies a covenant. This is why the Lodge requires the candidate to offer his oaths on the Masonic altar. The word *altar* appears in Sacred Scripture over five hundred times and invariably refers to the place on which sacrifices are offered to God. As the Masonic Bible tells us (p. 32), the Masonic altar, too, is a "place of sacrifice." When the candidate swears the oath at this altar, he is sacrificing his former religious beliefs for the new religious faith of Freemasonry. The bloody nature of the penalties seals the Masonic covenant into which he is now bound. He has taken on a new family and

---

[17] The word "covenant" comes from the Latin word *convenire*, which means "to come together."

is called "brother" for the first time. Immediately after the blood oath, the Worshipful Master instructs the Senior Deacon to "remove the cabletow from around *our brother* as he is now bound to us by a stronger tie" (emphasis added).[18] The newly made Mason is not only united in a sacred bond with his Masonic brothers but also in the doctrines of Freemasonry. This inviolable bond is called "the Mystic Tie" (Masonic Bible, p. 51).

The notion of a sacred and inviolable bond among men that is rooted, not in the sacramental life of the Church but in the generic teachings of the Lodge, is contrary to God's eternal plan in Jesus Christ. Through the sacrifice of Christ, God has chosen to gather all people together according to the Spirit (cf. Acts 10:35, 1 Cor 11:25). This Spirit is poured out in baptism, by which God makes all Christians brothers in his Son, Jesus Christ. The gift of baptism constitutes the foundation of communion among all Christians and the sacramental bond of unity existing among all who, through it, are reborn (cf. CCC 1271). Baptism also seals Christians with the indelible spiritual mark of belonging to Christ and enables them to serve God through the exercise of their baptismal priesthood (cf. CCC 1272-1273). Without this gift of divine sonship in Christ, the Masonic terminology "Fatherhood of God" and "brotherhood of man" is nothing more than the heresy of Modernism.

We are brethren, then, not by nature, but by the gift of grace, which allows us to share in the life of Christ (cf. CCC 654). This brotherhood is fully realized in the celebration of the Holy Eucharist, which unites all the faithful into one body — the Church (cf. CCC 1396). Just as Catholics are united to God through the Precious Blood Jesus offers in the Eucharist, Masons are bound to the brotherhood of Masonry by the symbolic blood they offer in the oaths.

---

[18] Wisconsin Multiple Letter Cipher, 41.

The brotherhood of those who have taken the Masonic oath is thus presented as a bond of unity superior to that shared by those baptized in Christ. Whether Christian or Hindu, Buddhist or Jew, all those yoked together by the Masonic oaths are brothers under the GAOTU. At the same time, men not initiated into the mysteries of the Lodge, Christian or not, are "profanes." Thus, the Christian Mason, if he is to be faithful to his Masonic oath, must look at uninitiated fellow Christians as outsiders. These oaths also place a wall of division between a Christian Mason and his wife. Though the two have become one flesh in Christ through the sacrament of marriage, the Mason is precluded from revealing any of the esoterica of the Lodge to his bride lest he be worthy of death.

Christians who have taken these improper oaths often wonder how to free themselves. Since Old Testament times, it has been recognized that rash oaths (whether to do good or bad) had to be confessed and the sin atoned for in order to restore communion with God (cf. Lev 5:4-6). Catholic Masons must renounce these oaths in the sacrament of penance (cf. John 20:21-23). Notwithstanding the mercy of God to free repenting sinners of these oaths, the Masonic Bible (p. 29) teaches that "a man may sever his connection with a Masonic Lodge, but it is utterly impossible for any Mason who has been honest and understanding in accepting the Rites of Freemasonry to repudiate his Masonic Obligations."

Enlightenment

After the oath is taken, the Worshipful Master asks the candidate what he most desires. The Senior Deacon whispers the response in the candidate's ear: "Light." After the candidate answers, the Worshipful Master declares to the lodge that he will now bring the newly made brother "from darkness to light." The brethren all make the Due Guard as the Worshipful Master recites the first three verses of Sacred Scripture — with a significant addition:

> In the beginning God created the heaven and the earth. And the earth was without form and void, and darkness was upon the face of the deep. And the Spirit of God moved upon the face of the waters. And God said, "Let there be light!" and there was light. In humble commemoration of that august event, I now say, Masonically, "Let there be Light."[19]

At this point, the candidate's hoodwink is removed by the Senior Deacon. The brethren clap loudly in unison, and then make the Sign. The new Mason discovers that he is kneeling at the Masonic altar with his hands placed upon the Volume of the Sacred Law along with the Square and Compasses, the "Great Lights of Masonry." The lodge room is dark. The only light comes from the three candles burning on the South side of the Masonic altar. These are called the three "Lesser Lights" of Masonry. The Apprentice sees the lodge brothers arrayed in two single-file lines in front of the altar, facing each other and looking at him.

The Worshipful Master approaches the altar and explains to the brother the secret mysteries of the Great and Lesser lights:

> The three Great Lights are the Holy Bible [if the candidate is Christian], Square and Compasses. The Holy Bible [or _____] is to rule and guide our faith; the Square to square our actions; and the compasses to circumscribe and keep us within due bounds with all mankind, more especially with a brother Mason.

> The three Lesser Lights are three burning tapers placed in a triangular form representing the sun, moon and Master

---

[19] Nevada Ritual, 20.

of the Lodge, because as the sun rules the day and the moon governs the night, so ought the Worshipful Master to endeavor to rule and govern his Lodge with equal regularity.[20]

After these explanations, the lights in the lodge room are turned back on and the brethren return to their places, except for the candidate and the Senior Deacon, who stands behind him. The Worshipful Master, having returned to his place in the East, teaches the brother the secret step of the Entered Apprentice, along with the Due Guard and Sign and their meanings. After this instruction, the Worshipful Master once again approaches the altar and, through a ritualistic exchange with the Senior Deacon, invests the brother with the grip of an Entered Apprentice, along with its secret name: *Boaz.*

All the anticipation of the first degree has led to this eureka moment of "enlightenment." But how is the Christian Mason enlightened? Though he has been told that the Bible is one of the Great Lights in Masonry, it has been presented in a symbolic context, as on par with the Square and Compasses. The Apprentice may even have been told that no Mason has to accept the Bible as God's inspired word. If the Christian Apprentice were to attend the initiation of a Hindu at the next meeting, the Vedas would be the Great Light. The explanation of the Lesser Lights of sun and moon and their ruling and governing authority — clear vestiges of pre-Christian astral worship — only adds confusion. Yet by virtue of his enlightenment, the Masonic Bible calls the new Mason a "son of light" (p. 49).

Even though the Mason is left to figure out the spiritual significance of his enlightenment for himself, he is made to feel that

---

[20] Wisconsin Multiple Letter Cipher, 1998, 41.

he possesses knowledge of light and truth that the uninitiated do not possess. By hearing that each Mason's personal religious judgments form the basis of light and truth, the new Mason begins to become conditioned to accept the religious subjectivism of Freemasonry.

The symbolic parallels between Masonic initiation and Christian baptism are apparent. While the Lodge teaches that men become sons of light through their initiation into Freemasonry, the Church teaches that men become "sons of light" through the sacrament of baptism. The *Catechism* says: "Having received in Baptism the Word, 'the true light that enlightens every man,' the person baptized has been 'enlightened,' he becomes a 'son of light,' indeed, he becomes 'light' himself" (CCC 1216).

The Church's usage of "son of light" describes, not the attainment of some subjective spiritual illumination, but our status as adopted sons of God who have become partakers of the divine nature, members of Christ and co-heirs with him, and temples of the Holy Spirit (cf. CCC 1265, 2782). By baptism, which is the Christian "bath of enlightenment" (cf. CCC 1216), the Christian becomes a member of the Body of Christ (cf. CCC 1267). As such, the person baptized belongs, no longer to himself, but to him who died and rose for us (cf. CCC 1269). The Lodge claims to bring its members from darkness to light in Masonic initiation, making them sons of light. The Lodge, however, ignores the only "true light that enlightens every man," Jesus Christ, the "light of the world" (Jn 1:9; 8:12; 9:5).

After the Entered Apprentice has been enlightened, he is instructed to rise and salute the Junior and Senior Wardens with the Due Guard and Sign. That done, the Apprentice receives additional teachings regarding the Masonic apron and Masonic charity. The Worshipful Master then orders that the brother be given back his clothing and returned to the lodge for further instruction.

Warnings

The newly made Mason is next instructed on the absolute necessity of concealing Masonry's teachings from the uninitiated. He "must be reserved in all that relates to the esoteric concerns of Masonry" (Masonic Bible, p. 28). The Entered Apprentice swears that he will never

> write, indite, print, paint, stamp, stain, hue, cut, carve, mark or engrave the same upon anything movable or immovable, whereby or whereon the least word, syllable, letter, or character may become legible or intelligible to myself or another, whereby the secrets of Freemasonry may be unlawfully obtained through my unworthiness.[21]

It is interesting to note that this most solemn requirement is universally violated. Grand Lodges usually print out the Masonic rituals and make them available to subsidiary lodges so that the brethren may learn them. Much of the ritual is written in plain English. The esoteric teachings, such as the passwords and oaths, may be printed in a ciphered format that, with some study, also becomes understandable. Thus, this string of prohibitions serves no real purpose other than to impress upon the initiate the secret nature of the Lodge's teachings. These "mysteries," the new Mason is told, "are to distinguish you from the rest of the community and mark your consequence among Masons."[22]

The Mason is also told that he should practice the virtues of temperance and fortitude, not in order to grow in holiness, but to equip himself with the ability to preserve the secrets of Masonry:

---

[21] Nevada Ritual, 19.

[22] Wisconsin Multiple Letter Cipher, 60.

[By temperance you] are thereby taught to avoid excess or the contracting of any licentious or vicious habits, the indulgence of which might lead you to disclose some of those valuable secrets which you have promised to conceal and never reveal, and which would consequently subject you to the contempt and detestation of all good Masons, if not to the penalty of your Obligation, that of having your throat cut across, your tongue torn out and with your body buried in the sands of the sea, at low-water mark, where the tide ebbs and flows twice in twenty-four hours.[23]

Every Mason must learn fortitude "as a safeguard or security against any illegal attack that may be made by force or otherwise to extort from him any of those valuable secrets with which he has been so solemnly entrusted."[24] The Masonic Bible also tells the Mason: "You shall be cautious in your words and carriage, that the most penetrating stranger shall not be able to discover or find out what is not proper to be imitated." Neglecting such a duty "becomes a heinous crime" (p. 37).

Freemasonry is also concerned with public perception and repeatedly charges the Mason not to stain the organization's reputation. Masons are taught to avoid arguing with those who oppose the institution: "Neither are you to suffer your zeal for the institution to lead you into argument with those who, through ignorance, may ridicule it."[25] When encountering "the enemies of Masonry," the brethren are reminded to practice the Masonic virtues of "silence and circumspection."[26] "Let us not dispute, argue, or engage in discussion on this subject of Anti-Masonry,"

---

[23] Nevada Ritual, 40-41.
[24] Wisconsin Multiple Letter Cipher, 56-57.
[25] Ibid., 60.
[26] Nevada Ritual, 149.

Alphonse Cerza reminds the brethren. "Let us continue to maintain a discreet silence."[27] Yet many zealous Masons ignore these exhortations, and aggressively and publicly defend the Lodge.

With regard to possible Masonic membership, Masons are also taught to be careful in evaluating prospective new members:

> If, in the circle of your acquaintance, you find a person desirous of being initiated into Masonry, be particularly careful not to give him encouragement unless you are convinced he will conform to our rules . . . that the honor, glory and reputation of the Institution may be firmly established and the world at large convinced of its good effect.[28]

Maintaining the secrecy of the doctrines and practices of Freemasonry is considered to be a Masonic Landmark, an essential element of the Craft. Pike calls Masonic secrecy "indispensable in a Mason of whatever degree."[29] The Masonic Bible directs Masons to punish "cowans," a Masonic word that means intruder. The term is "used especially of an eavesdropper . . . a person who seeks the secrets and benefits of Freemasonry in a clandestine manner, and when apprehended should be severely punished" (p. 26).

Masonry's emphasis on the secrecy of its teachings and practices appeals to many of the brothers. Things that are secret are often perceived as more attractive or more valuable than things that are not. But, after a bit of reflection, the Mason must admit that the Lodge has given him little of value, especially of spiritual and moral value. Yes, he has been invested with secret passwords and has gained some new friendships, but he has no greater insight into the mystery of God and the divine truths for which Freemasonry claims to search. To the contrary, if the Christian Mason had been

---

[27] *Let There Be Light: A Study in Anti-Masonry,* 55.

[28] Wisconsin Multiple Letter Cipher, 60.

[29] *Morals and Dogma,* 109.

lukewarm in his faith before becoming a Mason, the religious relativism of the Lodge will likely cause him further confusion.

Freemasonry's requirement of secrecy serves no real purpose other than to keep the public ignorant about its religious teachings. By emphasizing secrecy, the Lodge hopes to condition its members to believe they have been given special knowledge and that it is their duty to keep that knowledge secret. If Freemasonry made public its rituals and doctrines, its claim to be a fraternity would be severely compromised and new membership petitions would all but cease.

As this chapter demonstrates, Freemasonry initiates its members into a way of life shrouded in secrecy and mysticism quite distinct from anything found in Christian spirituality. By swearing morbid oaths to God before family and friends, being warned to maintain secrecy, and dealing with the possible dishonor of ever abrogating Masonic loyalty, it is no wonder why many Masons are reluctant to challenge the teachings of the Lodge, much less leave Freemasonry. By God's grace, however, more and more men are leaving the Lodge each year.

IS FREEMASONRY A RELIGION?

Having studied the various teachings and practices of the Lodge, we can safely conclude that Freemasonry is a religious institution. Mackey forthrightly affirms it:

> The tendency of all true Freemasonry is toward religion. . . .
> Look at its ancient landmarks, its sublime ceremonies, its
> profound symbols and allegories — all inculcating religious
> doctrine, commanding religious observance, and teaching
> religious truth, and who can deny that it is eminently a reli-
> gious Institution?[1]

Masonic ritual says that Masonry is "so far interwoven with religion as to lay us under obligations to pay that rational homage to the Deity, which at once constitutes our duty and our happiness."[2] Yet, while most American Masons acknowledge the religious nature of the Lodge, they emphatically deny that Freemasonry is a religion. Henry Wilson Coil, modern Masonry's top scholar, commented on this inconsistency:

> Some attempt to avoid the issue by saying that Freemasonry
> is not a religion but is religious, seeming to believe that the

---

[1] *Mackey's Revised Encyclopedia of Freemasonry*, Vol. 2, 847.
[2] Masonic Manual of the Grand Lodge of Georgia (1983), 36.

substitution of an adjective for a noun makes a fundamental difference. It would be as sensible to say that a man had no intellect but was intellectual or that he had no honor but was honorable. The oft repeated aphorism 'Freemasonry is not a religion' . . . has been challenged as meaningless, which it seems to be.[3]

Religion is generally defined as a belief in a superhuman power to be obeyed and worshiped as the Creator of the universe, which is expressed in conduct or ritual. To answer the question of whether or not Freemasonry is a religion, let us summarize some of the Lodge's characteristics that we have studied thus far. Freemasonry has its own

- religious doctrines (*immortality of the soul; bodily resurrection*);
- rituals which exemplify these doctrines (*Hiramic Legend; apron presentation*);
- prayers (*with special terminology such as "so mote it be"*);
- names and symbols for God (*GAOTU; letter* G; *All-Seeing Eye*);
- names and symbols for heaven (*celestial lodge above; clouded canopy*);
- soteriology (*purity of life and conduct necessary to gain admission into heaven*);
- burial rites (*prayers; depositing apron and sprig of acacia*);
- altar (*lodge furniture; displays of religious writings; oaths sworn here*);
- covenants (*the oaths with conditional self-curses*);
- chaplain (*a Blue lodge officer responsible for Masonic benediction*);
- vestments (*aprons; white gloves; jewels; collars; hats*);

---

[3] *Coil's Masonic Encyclopedia*, 512.

- meeting places (*lodges, also called temples*);
- consecration rites for lodges (*prayer; pouring oil over the Northeast corner*);
- music (*organist or soloist adds music to certain parts of the rituals*);
- calendar (*A.L. 6006 — "Anno Lucis" — versus A.D. 2006 — "Anno Domini"*);
- feast days (*St. John the Baptist on June 24; St. John the Evangelist on December 27*);
- Masonic authorities who say it is a religion (*books recommended by Grand Lodges*).

In light of these characteristics, we consider Coil's question and conclusion:

> Does Freemasonry continually teach and insist upon a creed, tenet, and dogma? Does it have meetings characterized by the practice of rites and ceremonies in and by which its creed, tenet, and dogma are illustrated by myths, symbols and allegories? If Freemasonry were not a religion, what would have to be done to make it such? Nothing would be necessary or at least nothing but to add more of the same.[4]

On the evidence of its own rituals, practices and spokesmen, Freemasonry is, objectively speaking, a religion.[5] In the words of

---

[4] *Coil's Masonic Encyclopedia*, 512.

[5] A California district court agreed. In *Two-thirty Three Club. v. Welch*, the court held that the activities of a Masonic lodge, which were predominantly to perform Masonic ritual and foster the civic and spiritual ideals of Freemasonry, were largely nonsocial, and the social and entertainment features were incidental only. Consequently, the lodge was not exempt from paying taxes on dues and membership fees that social, athletic or sporting club organizations were exempt from paying under state law. *Two-thirty Three Club v. Welch*, 2 F. Supp. 963, 1932 U.S. Dist. Lexis 1564; 12 A.F.T.R. (P-H) 617, (1932).

Albert Pike, "Every Masonic lodge is a temple of religion, and its teachings are instruction in religion."[6] Masonry is, in fact, a more formal and structured religion than many organizations that call themselves religions, including many nondenominational Christian churches, Christian Scientism, Seventh-day Adventism, Unitarianism, Buddhism, and Hinduism. Freemasonry is also considered more universal than many other religions. Think about this question: If American Masons began calling Freemasonry a religion, what would the Lodge be lacking to support their declaration?

To Christians — Catholics in particular — the Lodge does not appear to be a religion. The Catholic is accustomed to the sacramental liturgy of the Church. The worship may include music, singing, preaching, acclamations, incense, and a profession of faith. Most importantly, the worship is Christ-centered and is consummated in the breaking of the bread. Such distinctive worship is not found in the Lodge. Nevertheless, Coil says the difference between the Lodge and the Church is one of degree, and not kind: "Some think that, because it is not a strong or highly formalized or highly dogmatized religion such as the Roman Catholic Church, . . . [the Lodge] can be no religion at all. . . . The fact that Freemasonry is a mild religion does not mean that it is no religion."[7]

Catholics and other Christians may tend to view its rituals, not as parallel or competing with, but as subordinate and supplementary to, Christianity. The Lodge's use of Scripture passages from the New Testament in its rituals may foster such an impression. For the Christian Mason, if the Lodge is practicing religion, it is more like Christianity than anything else. Of course, Masonry's use of New Testament passages — always with references to Jesus carefully excised — is not to convey Christian ideas

---

[6] *Morals and Dogma*, 213.
[7] *Coil's Masonic Encyclopedia*, 512.

to its members. These passages are used to deceive the baptized into thinking the Lodge is Christian while conditioning them to accept the Masonic worldview of religious relativism. The Christian is repeatedly exposed to the Lodge's use of the Bible, dedications to the holy Saints John, and Christian religious terminology such as *enlightenment* and *resurrection*. The Christian Mason's familiarity with these elements tends to dull his misgivings and eventually leads to tolerance and acceptance. Through his continued participation in the religion of the Lodge, the Christian Mason is drawn ever so slowly away from his Master and Lord by the one who masquerades as an angel of light (cf. 2 Cor 11:14).

Albert Pike does not hide Masonry's intent to deceive its initiates:

> Masonry, like all the Religions, all the Mysteries, Hermeticism and Alchemy, conceals its secrets from all except the Adepts and Sages, or the Elect, and uses false explanations and misinterpretations of its symbols to mislead those who deserve only to be misled; to conceal the Truth, which it calls Light, from them, and to draw them away from it.[8]

In the same work, Pike shamelessly admits that the initiate "is intentionally misled by false interpretations. It is not intended that he shall understand them, but it is intended that he shall imagine he understands them. Their true explication is reserved for the Adepts, the Princes of Masonry."[9]

Martin L. Wagner, a scholar of Masonry, examined how the Lodge uses elements of Christianity to deceive its Christian members into accepting Masonic beliefs. Wagner commented in particular on Masonic terminology:

---

[8] *Morals and Dogma*, 104-105.
[9] Ibid., 819.

The peculiar theological religious ideas which Freemasonry holds and aims to inculcate, while positively non-Christian, are expressed in terms of Christian theology, not to express the Christian ideas or to show their harmony with Christian thought, but to give them a Christian coloring the more effectually to deceive, mislead and hoodwink the neophyte, the conscientious member and the non-Mason. . . . [M]any a Mason is misled by them, to believe that Freemasonry is a Christian institution.[10]

Albert Mackey also denies that the Lodge is an organization without a creed:

Although Freemasonry is not a dogmatic theology, and is tolerant in the admission of men of every religious faith, it would be wrong to suppose that it is without a creed. On the contrary, it has a creed, the assent to which it rigidly enforces, and the denial of which is absolutely incompatible with membership in the Order. This creed consists of two articles: First, a belief in God, the Creator of all things, who is therefore recognized as the Grand Architect of the Universe; and secondly, a belief in the eternal life, to which this present life is but a preparatory and probationary state.[11]

Pike explains that any tenets beyond Masonry's basic profession of faith are erroneous: "But Masonry teaches, and has preserved in their purity, the cardinal tenets of the old primitive faith, which underlie and are the foundation of all religions. All that ever existed have had a basis of truth; all have overlaid the truth with error."[12]

---

[10] *Freemasonry: An Interpretation*, 153.
[11] *An Encyclopedia of Freemasonry*, 192.
[12] *Morals and Dogma*, 161.

We could further formulate Freemasonry's creed vis-à-vis the Apostles' Creed as follows:

Apostles' Creed	Masonic Creed
I believe in God, the Father almighty,	I believe in God,
creator of heaven and earth.	the Creator of heaven and earth.
I believe in Jesus Christ, his only Son,	I believe in . . .
our Lord. He was conceived by	
the power of the Holy Spirit	
and born of the Virgin Mary.	
He suffered under Pontius Pilate,	
was crucified, died, and was buried.	
He descended into hell. On the	
third day he arose again. He ascended	
into heaven and is seated at the	
right hand of the Father. He will come	
again to judge the living and the dead.	
I believe in the Holy Spirit,	
the holy catholic Church,	
the communion of saints,	
the forgiveness of sins,	
the resurrection of the body,	. . . the resurrection of the body and life
and the life everlasting. Amen.	everlasting. Amen. So mote it be.

Although Freemasonry's belief in God and resurrection is consistent with the Catholic faith, it is not permissible for the faithful to distinguish between those articles of faith that are fundamental and those that are not. This would be saying that some elements of what God has revealed must be accepted, while others can be left to our discretion.[13] Pope Pius XI asks: "Are these truths not equally certain, or not equally to be believed . . . ? Has not God revealed them all?"[14]

While the Catholic faith is God's divine revelation to man, the religion of Freemasonry is man's human response to God. We would do well to heed St. Paul's warning to the Colossians: "See to it that no one makes a prey of you by philosophy and empty deceit, according to human tradition, according to the elemental spirits of the universe, and not according to Christ" (Col 2:8). And in the Second Letter of John (9), we are plainly told, "Any one who goes ahead and does not abide in the doctrine of Christ does not have God; he who abides in the doctrine has both the Father and the Son."

As Mackey states in his opus *An Encyclopedia of Freemasonry*, Freemasonry is a religion, and this religion is not Christianity (p. 619).

---

[13] Cf. Pope Pius XI, encyclical, *Mortalium Animos*, No. 9.
[14] Ibid.

Chapter

VII

FREEMASONRY AND THE CATHOLIC CHURCH

The Catholic Church has opposed the Lodge nearly since the birth of modern Freemasonry in 1717. Since the founding of the Grand Lodge of England, twelve popes have explicitly condemned Freemasonry or Masonic principles. These condemnations have taken the form of constitutions, encyclicals, and apostolic letters. Many of the pronouncements were issued in response to the anticlerical activities of the Grand Orient lodges of Europe and Latin America. Other pronouncements dealt with Masonry's desire for separation of Church and State. However, the Church's opposition to Masonry has focused primarily on the religious naturalism and indifferentism of the Lodge and on the immorality of the Masonic oaths. This section summarizes these pronouncements.

Papal Decrees

Clement XII

Pope Clement XII issued the Church's first condemnation of Freemasonry in 1738, in his constitution *In Eminenti*. Clement declared to all the faithful that the tenets of Freemasonry, to which a Mason swore on the Bible, were a threat to both the teachings of the Church and the stability of governments and society: "[T]hese same Societies, Companies, Assemblies, Meetings, Congregations or Conventicles of *Liberi Muratori* [Freemasons] . . . are to be condemned and prohibited, and by Our present constitution, valid forever, we do condemn and prohibit them." In this same document, Clement also extended the penalty of automatic excommunication to any of the faithful who joined Masonry or supported the Lodge in any way. The penalty could only be lifted at the hour of death by the Supreme Pontiff at that time. Clement's condemnations were repeated by eleven subsequent popes over the next two hundred years. The Masonic Bible describes Pope Clement by stating that "a more bitter persecutor of Masonry has not lived" (p. 26), and declares his condemnations to be "blasphemous and libelous to the utmost degree, preposterous and utterly false to the tenets and practices of the Order" (p. 13).

Benedict XIV

The purpose of Pope Benedict XIV's constitution *Providas* (1751) was to strengthen and confirm his predecessor's "most serious condemnations" (*gravissima damna*) of Freemasonry, noting that there were some who claimed the penalty of excommunication imposed in 1738 by Clement XII no longer carried force. Benedict declared: "We confirm, strengthen, renew that Constitution . . . just as if It had been published firstly by our own motion, by our authority and in our name, and we will and decree that it have perpetual force and efficacy." Benedict also reasserted that the doctrinal and moral errors of Masonry were the reasons for the Church's condemnation, and emphasized that Freemasonry threatened the purity of the Catholic religion. The Pope decried the Masonic oaths, which he said were contrary to the laws of the state and religion. Benedict declared that anyone who would oppose his approbation would "incur the wrath of Almighty God, and of His Blessed Apostles Peter and Paul."

Pius VI

In 1775, in his encyclical *Inscrutabile*, Pius VI wrote of the various dangers confronting the Church and the pontificate. These dangers included the "heretical sects" that view God as "idle and uncaring, making no revelation to men" and assert "that everything holy and divine is the product of the minds of inexperienced men smitten with empty fear of the future and seduced by a vain hope of immortality." Such "deceitful sages," said the Pope, "soften and conceal the wickedness of their doctrine with seductive words and statements; in this way, they attract and wretchedly ensnare many of the weak into rejecting their faith or allowing it to be greatly shaken." Although Pius VI does not mention Freemasonry explicitly in this encyclical, it has always been understood as a condemnation of Masonry and its principles.

Pius VII

Pius VII's letter *Ecclesiam Christi*, issued in 1821, reaffirmed the condemnations and focused on a new form of Masonry, the Carbonari, that was developing in Italy. The Pope noted that this sect met secretly, uniting men of any religion into the society, used heretical books and catechisms in secret meetings and ceremonial degrees, swore severe oaths promising never to reveal its principles to outsiders, boasted of its demand for the exercise of charity and virtue, and gave "to each one great license for devising by his own genius and from his own ideas for himself a religion which he may practice, once indifference to religion has been introduced." The Pope charged the Carbonari with "simulating" respect for the Catholic faith and Jesus Christ, but he warned that their ways of speaking are "more slippery than oil." Pius VII condemned the Carbonari, imposing again the penalty of automatic excommunication for any who would affiliate with them.

Leo XII

Pope Leo XII's encyclical *Quo Graviora*, issued in 1826, began by recalling how his predecessors understood and took action against the secret factions of men who contrive maliciously against Christ and his Church. Adding his own condemnation of Freemasonry, Leo declared invalid the "impious and accursed oath, by which they bind those who are received into these sects that they will reveal to none those things which pertain to those sects."

Addressing the question of whether Masonry's lower degrees were somehow exempt from the Church's condemnation, the Pope was absolutely clear:

> Have it for certain that no one can be a member of those sects, without being guilty of the most serious disgraceful act; and drive away from your ears the words of those who vigorously declare that you may assent to your election to the lower degrees of their sects, that nothing is admitted in those degrees which is opposed to reason, nothing which is opposed to Religion, indeed that there is nothing proclaimed, nothing performed which is not Holy, which is not Right, which is not Undefiled. Truly that abominable oath . . . which must be sworn even in that lower echelon, is sufficient for you to understand that it is contrary to Divine Law to be enlisted in those lower degrees, and to remain in them.

Pius VIII

In his encyclical *Traditi Humilitati* (1829), Pius VIII confirmed the previous condemnations of Freemasonry. In so doing, Pius VIII expressed sadness at "the numberless errors and the teachings of perverse doctrines which, no longer secretly and clandestinely, but openly and vigorously attack the Catholic faith" (No. 3). Rejecting the errors of indifferentism, he wrote that "Among these heresies belongs that foul contrivance of the sophists of this age who do not admit of any difference among the different professions of faith and who think that the portal of eternal salvation opens for all from any religion" (No. 4). Pius issued this caution regarding the Masonic Bibles that were being circulated:

> We must also be wary of those who publish the Bible with new interpretations contrary to the Church's laws. They skillfully distort the meaning by their own interpretation.... Furthermore, the Bibles are rarely without perverse little inserts to insure that the reader imbibes their lethal poison instead of the saving water of salvation. (No. 5)

Gregory XVI

Pope Gregory XVI's 1832 condemnation of Masonic principles focused on the moralization of religion and the indifferentism of the Lodge. In his encyclical *Mirari Vos*, Gregory strongly rejected the evil of indifferentism:

> This perverse opinion is spread on all sides by the fraud of the wicked who claim that it is possible to obtain the eternal salvation of the soul by the profession of any kind of religion, as long as morality is maintained. ... With the admonition of the apostle that "there is one God, one faith, one baptism," may those fear who contrive the notion that the safe harbor of salvation is open to persons of any religion whatever. They should consider the testimony of Christ Himself that "those who are not with Christ are against Him," and that they disperse unhappily who do not gather with Him.

Pius IX

Between 1846 and 1873, Blessed Pius IX issued five bulls condemning the errors of Masonic principles. In his 1846 encyclical, *Qui Pluribus,* Pius characterized the Masonic movement as "a very bitter and fearsome war against the whole Catholic commonwealth . . . stirred up by men bound together in a lawless alliance" (No. 4). In his condemnation, the Pope highlighted the errors of naturalism and rationalism. Regarding those who propagate such theories, the Pope (in *Qui Pluribus*, No. 5) had this to say:

> They claim for themselves without hesitation the name of "philosophers." They feel as if philosophy, which is wholly concerned with the search for truth in nature, ought to reject those truths which God Himself, the supreme and merciful creator of nature, has deigned to make plain to men as a special gift. . . . So, by means of an obviously ridiculous and extremely specious kind of argumentation, these enemies never stop invoking the power and excellence of human reason; they raise it up against the most holy faith of Christ, and they blather with great foolhardiness that this faith is opposed to human reason.

Like his predecessors, Pius IX warned the faithful about heretical Bibles:

> The commentaries which are included often contain perverse explanations; so, having rejected divine tradition, the doctrine of the Fathers and the authority of the Catholic Church, they all interpret the words of the Lord by their own private judgment, thereby perverting their meaning. As a result, they fall into the greatest errors. (No. 14)

Pius' 1853 encyclical *Inter Multiplices*, addressed to the bishops of France, is also considered a condemnation of Freemasonry.

The Pope reminded the bishops that "the most deadly foes of the Catholic religion have always waged a fierce war, but without success, against this Chair" (No. 7) and exhorted them "to drive off and eliminate all dissentions which the ancient enemy labors to sow" (No. 3). The Pope also indicted the pestilential books and magazines that "attack the foundations of faith, and weaken the most sacred dogmas of our religion" (No. 5).

In his 1863 encyclical *Quanto Conficiamur Moerore*, Pius IX censured the Masonic principle of indifferentism as "a very grave error entrapping some Catholics who believe that it is possible to arrive at eternal salvation although living in error and alienated from the true faith and Catholic unity" (No. 7).

In his 1864 encyclical *Quanta Cura*, Pius reaffirmed the earlier condemnations of Masonic and other secret societies. He also rejected naturalism as the impious and absurd principle that teaches human society to disregard religion or, at least, to fail to make distinctions between true religion and false ones.

In addressing the state of the Church in Italy, Germany, and Switzerland in his 1873 encyclical *Etsi Multa*, Pius IX once again strongly warned the faithful about the errors of Freemasonry: "For from these the synagogue of Satan is formed which draws up its forces, advances its standards, and joins battle against the Church of Christ" (No. 28). Pius urged the Church to "bring back those who have unhappily joined these sects" and to "expose especially the error of those who have been deceived or those who assert now that only social utility, progress, and the exercise of mutual benefits are the intention of these dark associations" (Nos. 28, 30). If there remained any doubt about the Church's sentiment toward American Freemasonry, the Pope stated that "these decrees refer not only to Masonic groups in Europe, *but also those in America and in other regions of the world*" (No. 30; emphasis added).

Leo XIII

In his encyclical *Etsi Nos*, issued in 1882, Pope Leo XIII addressed conditions in Italy. While not explicitly mentioning Freemasonry, the Pope said that Rome had been profaned by "temples" devoted to heresy and described a movement that seeks to "efface from the public institutions that Christian stamp and character which has always, and with good reason, been the seal of the glories of Italy" (Nos. 3, 2).

Any doubts about Leo XIII's opposition to Masonry ceased after the Pope issued *Humanum Genus* two years later, in 1884. This encyclical was entirely devoted to the condemnation of the Lodge. After reaffirming all of the previous condemnations of Masonry and Masonic principles, Leo forbade anyone to join the society, whose constitution he denounced as "contrary to law and right . . . pernicious no less to Christendom than to the State" (No. 9).

After addressing the impropriety of Masonic secrecy and oaths, Leo XIII took up the errors of naturalism, describing it as the denial of any "dogma of religion or truth which cannot be understood by the human intelligence," or rejection of "any teacher who ought to be believed by reason of his authority" (No. 12). While not denying that the Lodge did charitable works, Leo said that "the masonic federation is to be judged not so much by the things which it has done . . . as by the sum of its pronounced opinions" (No. 11). Consequently, the Pope ratified all of his predecessors' decrees against Freemasonry and issued this warning: "Let no man think that he may for any reason whatsoever join the Masonic sect, if he values his Catholic name and his eternal salvation as he ought to value them" (No. 31).

Leo also mentioned Freemasonry in his 1887 letter *Officio Sanctissimo*, in which he addressed the situation of the Church in

Bavaria. Exhorting the bishops to preserve sound doctrine and refute those who oppose it, the Pope revisited the Church's struggles against the evil of naturalism. Three years later, in 1890, Leo issued the encyclical *Dell'Alto dell'Apostolico Seggio,* which addressed Freemasonry in Italy. Again the Pope warned about the spread of Masonic ideals. In addition to the theological and moral problems previously addressed, new problems that were noted included the sect's intention to abolish religious instruction in schools and exclude Catholic or clerical elements from all public administrations. Leo condemned the "Masonic sect" as the influence that was out "to destroy the religion of Christ" (No. 11).

In his encyclical *Inimica Vis,* issued in 1892, Leo XIII sought to reinvigorate the Church's opposition to Freemasonry. Fearing complacency within the Church, the Pope warned that "the Masonic sect proceeds with greater boldness day by day," seeking to deprive the people of their Catholic faith, the origin and source of their greatest blessings (No. 3). Leo declared that the aim of the Masonic order was "to see the religion founded by God repudiated and all affairs, private as well as public, regulated by the principles of naturalism alone" (No. 8).

Leo XIII concluded that "it is not sufficient merely to be aware of the wiles of this vile sect: we must also war against it, using those very arms furnished by the divine faith which once prevailed against paganism" (No. 9). Leo also issued, in conjunction with *Inimica Vis,* a separate letter indicting Freemasonry (1892). Specifically addressed to the Italian people, *Custodi di Quella Fede* called Freemasonry "the implacable enemy of Christ and of the Church." In his letter, the Pope said: "We tore from the face of masonry the mask which it used to hide itself and We showed it in its crude deformity and dark fatal activity" (No. 2). While the encyclical was limited to addressing Masonry's deplorable effects in Italy, the Pope also addressed the Lodge's universal errors: "[T]he satanic intent of the persecutors has been to substitute naturalism for Christianity, the worship of reason for the worship of faith, so-called independent morality for Catholic morality, and material progress for spiritual progress" (No. 4).

Leo's condemnation was clear as he stated: "Remember that Christianity and masonry are essentially irreconcilable, such that to join one is to divorce the other" (No. 10). For those who joined Freemasonry "by some supreme misfortune," the Pope warned that they must separate from the Lodge or "remain separated from Christian communion and lose their soul now and for eternity" (No. 11). Leo also warned that "everyone should avoid familiarity or friendship with anyone suspected of belonging to masonry or to affiliated groups. . . . These men seek to reconcile Christ and Belial, the Church of God and the state without God" (No. 15).

Less than two years later, in 1894, Leo XIII addressed Freemasonry for the seventh time in his encyclical letter *Praeclara Gratulationis Publicae.* Describing Masonry, the Pope made this statement: "Under the pretense of vindicating the rights of man and of reconstituting society, it attacks Christianity; it rejects revealed Doctrine, denounces practices of Piety, the Divine Sacraments, and every Sacred thing as superstition." Leo also condemned Masonry's rejection of the Scriptures as divinely inspired. In his closing comments on Masonry, the Pope prayed: "May God in His Mercy bring to naught their impious designs; nevertheless, let all Christians know and understand that the shameful yoke of Freemasonry must be shaken off once and for all."

Pius X

St. Pius X's encyclical *Vehementer Nos* (1906) dealt primarily with the French law of separation of Church and State. Although it does not mention Freemasonry explicitly, the Pope speaks of "impious sects" whose aim is to " 'de-Catholicize' France" (No. 16).

Less than a year later, in 1907, Pius again wrote to the people of France concerning the separation of Church and State in his encyclical *Une Fois Encore*. In this letter, Pius mentions "Masonic congresses" specifically as among those groups who have waged war against the Church, seeking to "uproot at all costs" the Christian faith from the hearts of the faithful (No. 4).

Pius XI

In 1924, Pius XI affirmed the "condemnation of Associations" (issued by his predecessor Pius X) in his encyclical *Maximam Gravissimamque*. Addressed to the bishops of France, Pius XI referred to associations that espouse "the sense of feeling or ideal inimical or foreign to God and to religion," and stated unequivocally: "Whatever Pius X condemned, We condemn" (No. 17). While primarily focused on lay diocesan associations and Church-State relations, the encyclical has also been held as a condemnation of Masonic principles.

Closing Comment

The anti-Masonic pronouncements of so many popes make it evident that the Church has felt the threat of Freemasonry. Rarely has the Church spoken about a topic more frequently.[1] Masonic movements throughout Europe publicly challenged the Church's doctrine and attempted to undermine her ecclesiastical authority. Masonry in the United States during the early part of the twentieth century publicly exhibited similar anti-Catholic sentiment. From the decrees cited above, it is clear that the Church's opposi-

---

[1] Twelve different popes have collectively issued twenty-three separate condemnations of Freemasonry over a 245-year period, from the reign of Clement XII (1738) to John Paul II (1983). If we spread the number of condemnations evenly over this period of time, we would see the Church condemning Masonry about every ten years.

tion to the Lodge, both in America and other regions of the world, has been based primarily upon its threat to Catholic faith and morals. This threat, as Pius IX noted, exists not just in Europe but in America and other regions of the world. Historian William Whalen, in his report to the U.S. bishops' Committee for Pastoral Research and Practices, also makes this observation:

> Those who say that the church really directs her condemnation against the Grand Orient lodges must assume that the Vatican does not know that Freemasonry is English in origin and overwhelmingly English-speaking in membership. Of the estimated 6 million members in all the various types of Masonic lodges worldwide, about 4 million live in the United States, 750,000 in the United Kingdom, 250,000 in Canada, and 400,000 in Australia and New Zealand. Perhaps nine out of 10 Masons live in an English-speaking country.[2]

Canon Law and Related Developments

Although the basis for the Church's doctrinal and moral opposition to the Lodge has always been clear, many wonder about how the Church's law (canon law) serves to enforce the popes' decrees. This next section reviews the evolution of canon law on Freemasonry and the Church's most recent teachings against Masonic associations.

The 1917 and 1983 Codes of Canon Law

The Church's 1917 Code of Canon Law *(Codex Iuris Canonici)* was promulgated on May 27, 1917, and made effective May

---

[2] Whalen, "The Pastoral Problem of Masonic Membership," *Origins*, 15/6 (June 27, 1985), 86.

19, 1918. The 1917 law codified the condemnations and penalties of nearly two centuries of papal pronouncements. Canon
2335 reaffirmed the automatic excommunication of Catholic
Freemasons first declared by Clement XII:

> Those who lend their names to a masonic sect or other asso-
> ciation of the same kind who plot against the Church incur
> the penalty of excommunication resting simply in the Apos-
> tolic See.

Canon 2336 imposed additional penalties on clerics or religious who belonged to Freemasonry. These included suspension
for clerics and a loss of active and passive voice for religious. Other
canons also affected Catholic Masons: they were denied Christian
burial (c. 1240, §1,1°); the right to a Christian marriage (c. 1065,
§1); the ability to enter a valid novitiate (c. 542, §1); the right to
inscribe validly in a pious association of the lay faithful (c. 693,
§1); and, the right to receive the right of patronage (c. 1453, §1).

Under Canon 2335, Catholics had to meet two requirements
in order to incur automatic excommunication: first, they actually
had to enroll in a Masonic organization; second, the organization
had to be devoted to subverting the interests of the Church. The
first requirement was easy to establish, by either obtaining a membership roll from a lodge or proving a person's active participation. But because the American lodges of the twentieth century
were less subversive than European lodges, many questioned
whether the second requirement would be satisfied as it related to
American Masons.

This question became more pervasive in the wake of the Second Vatican Council (1962-65). After Vatican II, there was a
renewal in ecumenical dialogue with non-Christian religions.
While the council did not directly address Freemasonry, bishops
in England, France, and Scandinavia began to discuss the appli-

cation of Canon 2335 to Masons in general. An auxiliary bishop in France and an Italian priest also had discussions with Masonic Grand Lodges in their respective countries. Some began to have the impression that each bishop could determine whether or not a particular lodge was acting contrary to the interests of the Church in deciding whether or not the excommunication applied.

During this period, the Church was also revising the 1917 Code of Canon Law (the revised code would eventually become the 1983 Code of Canon Law, which is the current law of the Church). Canons 2335 and 2336 were abandoned. This led to further confusion among some bishops regarding whether the excommunication of Canon 2335 retained its force or whether the Church was changing her centuries-old position on Masonry. Cardinal Francis Seper, prefect of the Sacred Congregation for the Doctrine of the Faith, issued a letter to Cardinal John Krol of Philadelphia. Dated July 19, 1974, the letter stated that (1) the Holy See had repeatedly sought information from the bishops about contemporary Masonic activities directed against the Church; (2) there would be no new law on this matter, pending the revision of the code then under way; (3) all penal canons were to be interpreted strictly; and (4) the express prohibition against Masonic membership by clerics, religious, and members of secular institutes was reiterated.

Even though Cardinal Seper again affirmed the Church's prohibition against Masonry, some bishops interpreted his letter as suggesting that the local ordinary was expected to conduct an investigation to determine whether or not a particular Masonic lodge in his diocese conspired against the Church. If a lodge were found not to be conspiring against the Church, some bishops concluded that the excommunication of Canon 2335 would not apply. Cardinal Seper's letter provided no methodology for making such determinations. More importantly, his letter did not mention the Church's doctrinal and moral objections to Freemasonry on the grounds of religious indifferentism, syncretism, and improper oaths. As a result, many Catholic men between 1974 and 1981 joined the Lodge in good faith, often after consulting with their local bishop or his delegates.

As the revisions to the Code of Canon Law continued, the German Episcopal Conference (GEC) undertook the first in-depth investigation of Freemasonry after Vatican II. From 1974 to 1980, German Catholic bishops engaged in extensive dialogue with the United Grand Lodges of Germany. The GEC assigned three tasks to the participating bishops: (1) to see if changes had taken place in Freemasonry, (2) to examine whether membership in the Catholic Church was compatible with membership in Freemasonry, and (3) to prepare society with the media of social communication in the case of a positive reply to the first two inquiries.

After six years of studying Masonic rituals and doctrines, the bishops unequivocally concluded that neither the principles of Freemasonry nor its self-definition had changed. While Masonry's humanitarian interests and charitable works were noted, the differences between Catholics and Masons in the area of religious doctrine were as opposed to one another as ever. The bishops' report confirmed that "simultaneous membership of the Catholic Church and of Freemasonry is impossible."[3] In support of their conclusion, the bishops listed twelve areas of Masonic teaching that are irreconcilable with Catholic faith:[4]

1. *The Masonic worldview.* Masons promote freedom from dogmatic adherence to any specific set of revealed truths.

---

[3] Cf. William J. Whalen, *Christianity and American Freemasonry,* 144; cf. "The Pastoral Problem of Masonic Membership," *Origins,* 15/6 (June 27, 1985), 92.

[4] Cf. Ronny E. Jenkins, "The Evolution of the Church's Prohibition against Catholic Membership in Freemasonry," *The Jurist* (Summer 1997), 741-43.

2. *The Masonic notion of truth.* Masons deny the possibility of objective truth.

3. *The Masonic notion of religion.* Masonic teaching propounds the notion that religions are all concurrently seeking the truth of the Absolute.

4. *The Masonic notion of God.* The Masons' deistic notion of God excludes any personal knowledge of the deity.

5. *The Masonic notion of God and revelation.* The deistic notion of God precludes the possibility of God's self-revelation to mankind.

6. *Masonic toleration.* The Masons promote a principle of toleration regarding ideas. Such a principle threatens not only the Catholic position, which holds for objective truth, but also the respect due to the Church's teaching office.

7. *Masonic rituals.* The rituals of the first three Masonic degrees exhibit a clear sacramental character, indicating that a significant transformation is undergone by those who participate in them.

8. *The perfectibility of humankind.* Masonic rituals have as an end the perfection of humankind. Masonry claims to provide all that is necessary to achieve this goal. Thus, the justification of a person through the work of Christ has no part in the struggle for perfection.

9. *Masonic spirituality.* Masonry makes a total claim on the life of its members. True adherence to the Christian faith is thereby jeopardized by the primary loyalty demanded by the Masonic Order.

10. *Divisions within Masonry.* Freemasonry is composed of lodges with varying degrees of adherence to Christian teaching. But even those lodges made up of Christian members seek to adapt Christianity to the Masonic worldview.

11. *Masons and the Catholic Church.* Even lodges that would welcome the Church's members as their own are not compatible with Catholic teaching.
12. *Masons and Protestants.* A 1973 meeting of Protestant churches determined that Protestants could decide whether to be members also of the Freemasons. But it warned that those Christians must always take care not to discount the necessity of grace for one's justification before God.

During the German bishops' investigation of Freemasonry, the revisions to the 1917 Code of Canon Law proceeded. In 1977, the canon that was proposed to replace Canon 2335 read as follows:

One who joins an association which plots against the Church is to be punished with a just penalty; one who promotes or moderates such an association is to be punished with an interdict.

This new formulation did not expressly provide for an excommunication, although a "just penalty" or an "interdict" could have the same ramifications. The proposed canon also did not expressly mention Masons, thus causing further confusion regarding the status of Catholic Masons.

To clarify the matter, Cardinal Seper issued on February 17, 1981, another letter from the Sacred Congregation for the Doctrine of the Faith. The cardinal acknowledged that his letter of July 19, 1974, had given rise to "erroneous and tendentious interpretations," and made clear that (1) his original letter did not in any way change the force of the existing Canon 2335; (2) the stated canonical penalties were in no way abrogated; and (3) he was but recalling the general principles of interpretation to be applied by the local bishop for resolving cases of individual persons, which was not to say that any episcopal conference now had the competence to pass judgment of a general character on the nature of Masonic associations in such a way as to derogate from the previously stated norms.[5]

Despite Cardinal Seper's clarifications and support of Church teaching, the debate regarding the status of Catholic Masons continued. In October 1981, the commission responsible for promulgating the new Code of Canon Law met to discuss whether or not to include an explicit condemnation of Freemasonry. By a vote of 31-13, with 15 abstentions, the commission decided not to mention Masons in the canon specifically. Instead, the matter of excommunication was left to the determination of local legislators.

The commission's decision was based on what it believed to be the varying character of Masonic lodges throughout the world. The commission, however, focused on the subversive nature of the lodges (which varied), not on the religious errors promoted by the lodges (which did not vary). Notwithstanding centuries of Church teaching on the incompatibility of Freemasonry with Catholic faith, the commission, inexcusably, did not adequately understand this doctrinal and moral incompatibility as it made its decisions about the substitute for Canon 2335.

The 1983 Code of Canon Law also reduced the number of offenses for which excommunication was applied from thirty-seven to seven. The elimination of an express excommunication for Catholic Masons was therefore borne, not from a new view of Freemasonry, but from a renewed emphasis on bringing those who separated themselves from the Church by sin back into her fold. These revisions, as we will see, also did not mean that Catholic Masons would no longer be subject to the penalty of excommunication as a result of their membership in Freemasonry.

---

[5] CDF, "Clarification Concerning Status of Catholics Becoming Freemasons" (February 17, 1981).

The proposed canon was published in January 1983 and became Canon 1374 in November of that year. Between its publication and its taking effect, doubts continued to be raised concerning its meaning and intent. For example, Canon 1374 inflicts penalties only on associations that plot against the Church. In light of the Church's historical opposition to Masonry on the grounds of faith and morals, plotting against the Church could reasonably include the propagation of erroneous teachings that might spiritually harm her members. But the canon provides no specific guidance on this question. Further, the just penalty and interdict, while harmful to the Catholic's communion with the Church, differ from the automatic excommunication simply reserved to the Holy See.

Declaration on Masonic Associations

Because of the changes in the new Code of Canon Law regarding Masons, the Congregation for the Doctrine of the Faith issued its "Declaration on Masonic Associations" on November 26, 1983, the day before the code became effective. This document, which was written by Cardinal Joseph Ratzinger (the future Pope Benedict XVI) and approved by Pope John Paul II, declares that Masonic principles are irreconcilable with the doctrine of the Church, and that Catholic membership in Freemasonry remains forbidden. The document further declares that Catholics who enroll in Masonic associations are in a state of grave sin and cannot receive the Eucharist.

The declaration also explains that the new code's failure to mention Masons explicitly was due to principles that guided the revision of the law. It also reiterates that a local bishop does not have authority to make a judgment on a Masonic lodge contrary to the congregation's declaration. Following is the full text of the declaration:

It has been asked whether there has been any change in the Church's decision in regard to Masonic associations since the new Code of Canon Law does not mention them expressly, unlike the previous Code.

This Sacred Congregation is in a position to reply that this circumstance is due to an editorial criterion which was followed also in the case of other associations likewise unmentioned inasmuch as they are contained in wider categories.

Therefore, the Church's negative judgment in regard to Masonic associations remains unchanged since their principles have always been considered irreconcilable with the doctrine of the Church and therefore membership in them remains forbidden. The faithful who enroll in Masonic associations are in a state of grave sin and may not receive Holy Communion. It is not within the competence of local ecclesiastical authorities to give a judgment on the nature of Masonic associations which would imply a derogation from what has been decided above, and this in line with the Declaration of this Sacred Congregation issued on 17 February 1981 (cf. AAS 73 [1981] pp. 240-241).

In an audience granted to Cardinal Ratzinger, the Supreme Pontiff John Paul II approved and ordered the publication of this Declaration which had been decided in an ordinary meeting of the Sacred Congregation.

Rome, from the Office of the Sacred Congregation for the Doctrine of the Faith, November 26, 1983.

This is the Church's most recent teaching regarding Catholic membership in Freemasonry. It reaffirms the Church's centuries of opposition to Masonry on grounds of faith and morals. While this declaration is not an authentic interpretation of canon law, it is a doctrinal and moral judgment concerning Catholic participation in Freemasonry rendered by the congregation that has the special competence to promote and safeguard the integrity of Catholic faith and morals (as well as having been written by a future pope of the Catholic Church). Catholics are therefore bound to follow the declaration in order to maintain communion with the Church.

While the letter does not interpret the 1983 Code of Canon Law, its declaration that Catholic Masons are, objectively speaking, in a state of grave sin exposes Catholic Masons to a variety of canonical penalties including, potentially, those provided under Canon 1374. For example, a Catholic Mason who is aware that the Church authoritatively judges membership in Freemasonry to be gravely sinful must not approach Holy Communion (Canon 916). This is simply the duty of all grave sinners to avoid a sacrilegious communion. Such a Catholic Mason who is aware of the grave sin must receive absolution in a sacramental confession before being able to receive Holy Communion again, unless there is a grave reason and no opportunity to confess (Canon 916). In order for his confession to be valid, the Catholic Mason must renounce his Masonic membership.

Because membership in Freemasonry is an external, public condition, the Catholic Mason can be refused Holy Communion by the pastors of the Church for obstinately persevering in his Masonic membership (Canon 915). Such a person would also be forbidden from receiving the anointing of the sick (Canon 1007), as well as from ecclesiastical funeral rites if public scandal were to result (Canon 1184, §1, °3).

Catholic Masons are subject to these sanctions only if they obstinately persevere in the sin. Obstinate perseverance means that the Catholic Mason chooses to disregard the warning of his pastor or other authority to terminate his Masonic affiliation. This was the case, for example, in the Diocese of Lincoln, Nebraska, where Bishop Fabian Bruskewitz excommunicated Catholic Masons, though only after giving them a warning about their Masonic affiliation and a period of time to make a decision about their continued membership in Freemasonry.

In addition, if the Catholic Mason does not act in a gravely imputable way, any canonical penalties that would otherwise apply would be mitigated or even eliminated (Canon 1321, §1). For example, if a Catholic Mason were invincibly ignorant about the Church's opposition to Freemasonry, he would not be subject to a penalty (Canon 1323, °2). If a Catholic Mason were aware of the Church's position against Freemasonry, was warned about it, and still continued with his membership, the canonical penalties would apply.

Canon 1364, which imposes automatic excommunication on apostates, heretics, and schismatics, applies to Catholic Masons as well. Canon 751 defines these terms:

> Heresy is the obstinate denial or obstinate doubt after the reception of baptism of some truth which is to be believed by divine and Catholic faith; apostasy is the total repudiation of the Christian faith; schism is the refusal of submission to the Supreme Pontiff or of communion with the members of the Church subject to him.

Heresy, apostasy, and schism are grave offenses against revealed truth and ecclesial communion. If a Catholic Mason embraced the theology of the Lodge (indifferentism, syncretism), he would be in heresy. If a Catholic Mason adamantly and persistently refused to acknowledge the Pope's authority to preclude his Masonic membership, he may also find himself in schism. These offenses automatically excommunicate the Catholic Mason from the Church. But, as with the other canons, the Catholic

Mason would have to act in a gravely imputable way, with full knowledge, deliberation, and persistence. Most Catholic Masons would probably not meet these requirements (but, in my personal experience, a fair number of Catholic Masons *do* meet these requirements). This analysis demonstrates that Catholic Masons are subject to a variety of canonical penalties, including excommunication, even if their lodges are not considered to be "plotting against the Church." William Whalen, who was commissioned by the Pastoral Research and Practices Committee to assist with the Church's study of Freemasonry, comments:

> If we try to make "plotting against the church" the sole criterion for allowing or disallowing membership, we in effect are saying that we do not concern ourselves with the nature of an organization or what it teaches. By the same token, we should allow membership by Catholics in organizations of spiritualists, theosophists and occultists so long as these groups do not plot against the church. But the church's historic stand has not been based primarily on whether Masonic lodges are hostile or neutral toward the church, but on the principles for which the lodge stands.[6]

The Catholic Mason should take away two important points from this discussion about the Church's canon law and Freemasonry. The first is that the Church's opposition to Freemasonry on the grounds of faith and morals is settled. Catholics who enroll in the Lodge are declared to be in a state of mortal sin and may not receive Holy Communion. This is the most detrimental effect of Catholic affiliation in Masonry. "Truly, truly, I say to you, unless you eat the flesh of the Son of man and drink his blood, you have

---

[6] "The Pastoral Problem of Masonic Membership," *Origins*, 15/6 (June 27, 1985), 87.

no life in you" (Jn 6:53; cf. 1 Cor 11:27). Those Catholic Masons who continue to receive the Eucharist in defiance of the Church's declaration are committing sacrilege and increasing the gravity of their spiritual condition. "Whoever, therefore, eats the bread or drinks the cup of the Lord in an unworthy manner will be guilty of profaning the body and blood of the Lord" (1 Cor 11:27).

The second point is that there is a significant distinction between the moral law and canon law. This is important for those Catholic Masons who justify their continued participation in Freemasonry based upon their perception of ambiguities in canon law, without addressing the Church's doctrinal and moral prohibitions against the Lodge. The moral law is unchanging because it has been given to us by God. Canon law, while grounded in the divine and moral law, does change in order to adapt to the human condition. It seeks to interpret the divine law in light of the historical moment. The 1983 code provided a great example of this change when it substantially reduced the number of offenses subject to excommunication.

The distinction was emphasized by the United States bishops' Committee for Pastoral Research and Practices in its confidential report on Freemasonry. The report was based on a study of Freemasonry after the enactment of the 1983 Code of Canon Law:

> What is at stake is the distinction between penal law and morality. . . . Not everything that is immoral is penalized in the church. Nor can one conclude from the fact that penal law does not cover some sin or that it is removed from it (or changed), that it is permissible to commit it. A clear example of this is abortion. Even if the excommunication were removed from abortion, it would still be wrong. Similarly, even if the excommunication was removed from joining an

organization that plotted against the church, it would still be wrong to join such an organization.[7]

The United States bishops concluded that the principles and basic rituals of American Masonry embody a naturalistic religion, active participation in which is incompatible with Christian faith and practice. Therefore, even though canonical penalties will depend upon the facts and circumstances, it is morally wrong for a Catholic to join Freemasonry because its principles are irreconcilable with those of the Catholic faith.

The Catholic Church is not the only church to oppose the Lodge. Whalen's report to the U.S. bishops provides a list:

> Other groups hostile to lodge membership include many branches of Lutheranism, the Christian Reformed Church, most Pentecostals, the Church of the Nazarene, the Seventh-day Adventists, the Holiness churches, the Quakers, the United Brethren in Christ, the Mennonites, the Free Methodists, the Church of the Brethren, the Assemblies of God, the Wesleyans, the Regular Baptists, the Salvation Army and significant minorities in such mainline churches as the Episcopal. Jehovah's Witnesses and the Church of Jesus Christ of Latter-day Saints [Mormons] also oppose Masonry.[8]

An Anglican priest who later converted to Catholicism summarized it best in his excellent book on Freemasonry, *Darkness Visible*: "No church that has seriously investigated the religious teachings and implications of Freemasonry has ever yet failed to condemn it."[9]

---

[7] "Masonry and Naturalistic Religion," *Origins*, 15/6 (June 27, 1985), 83.

[8] "The Pastoral Problem of Masonic Membership," *Origins*, 15/6 (June 27, 1985), 90. James B. Earley, chancellor for the Diocese of Scranton, provided a similar list in his 1998 notice on Freemasonry.

[9] Walton Hannah, *Darkness Visible*, 78.

Chapter

VIII

THE MASONIC CONSPIRACY

Introduction

Masonic content, ritual, and practice demonstrate that Freemasonry is a religion, and the Church has rightly condemned it on the grounds that Masonry's teachings are incompatible with Christian faith and morals. But this book would not be complete without addressing the impact that Masonic ideology has had on our society. Freemasonry has fought relentlessly to get rid of the Christian beliefs on which America was founded, and to usher in its nonsectarian worldview.[1] The Masonic movement has worked to prevent public busing of children to parochial schools, fought against released time for religious education in public schools, and resisted all forms of religious expression in public schools. Masonry has campaigned to block federal, state, and local aid to private schools. The historical record clearly shows that the aim of Freemasonry has long been to de-Christianize our society.

Traditional Views of Religion and Christianity

During the debates in the Constitutional Convention, the word *religion* was understood by the Framers to mean the duty we owe

---

[1] For more on this, I recommend Paul Fisher's *Behind the Lodge Door*.

to the Creator and the manner of discharging it. The Framers wanted to encourage that duty. To that end, the First Amendment to the United States Constitution was added. Known as the "establishment clause," it reads, in part: "Congress shall make no law respecting an establishment of religion, or prohibiting the free exercise thereof." From 1789 until the 1940s, the national record in support of religion in general — and Christianity in particular — is well documented.

The Founding Fathers intended that the clause preclude the federal government's establishing a single religion and enforcing the observation of it. At the same time, however, the Fathers agreed that religion was extremely important to American society and that the government should protect the people's right to practice it freely. Moreover, the records of the House debate clearly show that the government would not patronize those who professed no religion at all, viewing such persons with negativity. Recall that the U.S. Constitution closes with these words: "Done in Convention . . . the seventeenth day of September, *in the year of our Lord*, one thousand seven hundred and eighty seven" (emphasis added).

Federal legislation continued the establishment clause's purpose of encouraging religion in American life. For example, sections of territorial land sold by the government were reserved for schools and religious purposes. The Act of June 1, 1796, regulated land grants appropriated for the Society of the United Brethren for Propagating the Gospel Among the Heathens. In fact, the national policy on land grants for education between 1820 and 1865 placed no restriction on participation by private or religious schools. The government had also made contracts with sectarian schools for the education of the Indians and distributed funds to mission schools in the Catholic, Episcopalian,

Moravian, Presbyterian, Swedish Evangelical, and Reformed Episcopal traditions.

The Supreme Court in its early opinions identified the United States as a Christian nation. In *Vidal v. Girard's Executors* (1844), the court stated about Christianity that "its divine origin and truth are admitted, and therefore it is not to be maliciously and openly reviled and blasphemed against, to the annoyance of believers or the injury of the public."

In *Church of the Holy Trinity v. U.S.* (1892), the Supreme Court emphasized that America is a religious nation. The court also cited language from an opinion by Chancellor Kent, the chief justice of the New York Supreme Court in the case of *People v. Ruggles*: "[W]e are a Christian people, and the morality of the country is deeply ingrafted upon Christianity."

Mormon Church v. U.S. (1889) addressed the question of polygamy. After declaring it "a blot on our civilization," the high court said that "it is contrary to the spirit of Christianity and of the civilization which Christianity has produced in the Western world." In *Bradfield v. Roberts* (1899), the court held that the Constitution permitted the government to contract with corporations affiliated with the Catholic Church, which performed public welfare services. In *Pierce v. Society of Sisters* (1925), the court ruled unconstitutional an Oregon law requiring every child in that state to attend public school.

In 1865, Supreme Court Justice Joseph Story, a constitutional law scholar whose writings had a significant impact on American jurisprudence and the early court, made this comment:

> [I]t is impossible for those who believe in the truth of Christianity as a divine revelation to doubt that it is the especial duty of government to foster and encourage it among all the

citizens and subjects. This is a point wholly distinct from
that of the right of private judgment in matters of religion,
and of the freedom of public worship according to the dictates of one's conscience.[2]

The foregoing is a formidable historical record of our government's view of Christianity and its role in American life —
before the influence of Freemasonry.

Masonic Movement Toward Secularization

As the government sought to buttress Christian principles in
American society, Freemasonry fought for secularization. The
Scottish Rite was particularly vociferous in its efforts for de-Chris-
tianization. In 1915, it urged that graduates of American public
schools be given "preference in every appointment to public
office." In 1920, the Supreme Council of the Scottish Rite developed a comprehensive education plan that required sending all
children to public schools for a certain number of years. The Scottish Rite plan urged the establishment of a national department of
public education and recommended that teachers and textbooks
be carefully selected in order to exclude "sectarian propaganda." In
1922, both the Supreme Council and the Imperial Council of the
Nobles of the Mystic Shrine successfully lobbied for the passage of
legislation outlawing Catholic and other parochial schools in Oregon. This law was declared unconstitutional by a non-Masonically
controlled U.S. Supreme Court in the *Pierce* decision of 1925.

Freemasonry earnestly prosecuted its agenda for secularizing
America over the next two and a half decades. The Scottish Rite,
whose membership included many Supreme Court justices, U.S.
presidents, and other high government officials, led the effort.

---

[2] *Commentaries on the Constitution of the United States*, Vol. 2, 722.

Masonry's voice for secularization primarily came through its periodical *New Age,* a magazine published by the Scottish Rite of the Southern Jurisdiction. (In 1990, the Scottish Rite changed the name of its magazine to the *Scottish Rite Journal* to avoid unwanted publicity about its New Age ideologies).

The *New Age* boldly proclaimed the Craft's objective of imposing its views on society. Albert Pike, the Father of Scottish Rite Masonry, claimed that "[i]t is in the province of Masonry to teach all truths, not moral truth alone, but political and philosophical, and even religious truth."[3] More than a century ago, Pope Leo XIII recognized that Masonry's aim was "to make itself felt in all the circumstances of social life, and to become master and controller of everything."[4]

The *New Age* also did not hide its antipathy toward the Catholic Church.[5] As it pursued its goal of the de-Catholicization of society, it referred to the "insidious force of the Vatican Church-State." It also said that Catholicism, not communism or socialism, was the real threat to society and that Catholics should "repudiate" the anti-democratic doctrines of their Church. The Catholic presence on the House Committee on Education did frustrate Masonry's efforts to nationalize education and dominate the minds of American children. In 1935, eight of the fifteen members of this committee were Catholic.

In the 1930s, Freemasonry put its movement to secularize America into high gear. Beginning in 1935 and continuing

---

[3] *Morals and Dogma*, 148.

[4] Encyclical, *Dall'Alto dell'Apostolico Seggio* (October 15, 1890), No. 6.

[5] Nor does Scottish Rite ritual. The 30th degree of the Southern Jurisdiction denounces the Pope while participants perform the sacrilege of stabbing a skull adorned with the "tiara of the cruel and cowardly Pontiff," and the candidate exclaims, "Down with imposture! Down with crime!" The degree concludes with the participants stomping on the papal crown.

through the mid-1940s, the *New Age* carried out an extensive campaign against governmental assistance to sectarian institutions. From May 1935 to December 1946, the *New Age* published thirteen articles opposing state assistance for transportation and other aid for children who attended Catholic or other parochial schools. The *New Age* also published nine articles from 1940 to 1948 proclaiming Masonry's opposition to religion in public schools, including prayer and Bible reading. The Scottish Rite's campaign against religion in school also included opposition to released time for religious instruction of children. The *New Age* published seventeen articles from 1941 to 1946 expressing its disdain for such instruction in public schools.

Freemasonry also began publicly pressing its interpretation of the Constitution's establishment clause. Its aim was to get justices on the high court who would interpret the clause according to the Masonic worldview. To that end, President Franklin D. Roosevelt, a powerful member of the Craft, in his January 6, 1937, Message to Congress said, "The vital need is not an alteration of our fundamental law, but an increasingly enlightened view in reference to it." "Enlightened view," of course, meant a view illumined by Masonic principles. President Roosevelt made this remark as he was getting ready to pack the Supreme Court with Masons. Justice Robert H. Jackson, another ardent Freemason, also wrote that the Constitution and its amendments "are what the judges say they are." The Craft was gearing up for Masonic activism on the bench to separate the Church from the State.

In November 1935, the *New Age* published a commentary opposing aid to parochial schools. In it, the Craft reasoned that its position was supported by certain statements made by James Madison in his "Memorial and Remonstrance." In April 1937, Elmer Rogers, editor of the *New Age,* appeared as a witness before the House Committee on Education. Brother Rogers spoke out against legislation that would authorize federal funds for education, saying the Fraternity feared that some of the funds could be diverted to Catholic schools. In support of the Craft's position, Rogers also referred to Madison's "Memorial and Remonstrance."

Rogers also mentioned four Supreme Court decisions that, in his view, found state aid to sectarian institutions unconstitutional. These cases were *Watson v. Jones, Davis v. Beason, Reynolds v. U.S.,* and *Reuben Quick Bear v. Leupp.* In April 1940, the *New Age* published another editorial, "Strange Times Have Come," on its opposition to aid for sectarian endeavors, citing both Madison's "Memorial and Remonstrance" and Jefferson's Bill for Establishing Religious Freedom. That same year, the Fraternity vehemently opposed a congressional proposal to allow states to make available to parochial schoolchildren services of health, welfare, books, reading materials, or transportation that would be available for public schoolchildren.

Masonry's appeal to these authorities was a weak attempt to justify its secular views. Both Madison's "Memorial and Remonstrance" (1785) and Jefferson's Bill for Establishing Religious Freedom (1786) concerned religious freedom in Virginia only, and were written several years prior to the proposal and ratification of the establishment clause. Moreover, neither document was discussed during the debates in the Constitutional Convention, nor were they ever mentioned by any congressional leaders when the establishment clause was being drafted.

The *Reynolds* and *Beason* cases dealt with bigamy and polygamy. The Supreme Court's decisions against these practices demonstrated only that there are constitutional limits to the free exercise of religion. The *Reynolds* and *Beason* decisions strongly supported the Christian, not the secular, view of marriage. *Reynolds* defined *religion* as "the duty we owe the Creator." The *Watson* case dealt with property rights of religious societies, and the court ruled that it had no jurisdiction over questions of church discipline. *Reuben Quick Bear*, which noted that public appropriation for Indian education was constitutionally permissible, was also not on point.

While Masonry's campaign to laicize American schools pressed on, the government continued to favor public aid for private religious interests. This brought Masonry face-to-face with two problematic pieces of proposed legislation. The first was the Servicemen's Readjustment Act of 1944, or G.I. Bill of Rights, which provided a wide range of benefits for veterans, including money that could be used for tuition at religiously affiliated schools. The Craft was outraged. Although American Freemasonry always publicly avowed its patriotism, the Scottish Rite robustly fought against assistance to the men and women of our armed forces. This was Masonic hypocrisy at its worst. The G.I. Bill of Rights, nonetheless, received unanimous support in both the House and the Senate. It became law in June 1944.

The second piece of proposed legislation Masonry vigorously fought against was the Mead-Aiken bill, which proposed federal funding for parochial schools. Before this bill was actually formulated, a House Education committee, in December 1944, recommended federal funds for private colleges and universities. In January 1945, the National Education Association — an organization closely tied to the Scottish Rite — sponsored legislation that provided funding for public education but was silent regarding funding for private education. The bill (S 181) was principally sponsored by Democratic Senator Lister Hill of Alabama, a Mason.

Elmer Rogers, editor of the *New Age*, believed that Hill's proposal did not go far enough. On January 31, 1945, Rogers appeared before the Senate Education and Labor Committee to oppose S 181 on the ground that it did not give assurance that parochial schools could not receive federal benefits. Rogers even referred to certain portions of Pope Leo XIII's encyclical letter *Humanum Genus* in an attempt to show that the teachings of the Catholic Church were incompatible with the United States Constitution. Rogers failed to mention that *Humanum Genus* was a scathing condemnation of Freemasonry.

Soon after these hearings, Senators James Mead (D-NY) and George Aiken (R-VT) introduced education bill S 717, the Mead-Aiken bill, which expressly provided aid to parochial schools. Freemasonry viewed this new measure as dangerous. Rogers, in an article published in the *Scottish Rite News Bulletin* on April 5, 1945, wrote that the bill's "scheme to make public funds available to sectarian schools treats with contempt the principles set forth in Madison's Memorial of 1784 and the same principles affirmed later by Thomas Jefferson in his Act for Religious Freedom in the Legislature of Virginia, to say nothing of the curse that sectarian schools supported by public funds has inflicted upon man."

Justice Hugo L. Black, another powerful Scottish Rite Mason, also opposed the Mead-Aiken bill. He even wrote letters to brothers Hill and Rogers, expressing his concern that the pending legislation was contrary to the principles of Freemasonry, and inquired whether the Scottish Rite Supreme Council had taken a position against federal aid to education.[6] He wrote a similar letter to A. B. Andrews, a high Masonic official at the Scottish Rite temple in Birmingham, Alabama.[7] Justice Black also reminded his brethren of the five educational principles favored by the Supreme Council of the Scottish Rite. The first principle calls for American public schools to be "non-partisan, non-sectarian, efficient, democratic, for all of the children of all of the people." The fifth principle demands "entire separation of Church and State, and

---

[6] Cf. Paul Fisher, *Behind the Lodge Door*, 146-47.
[7] Ibid.

opposition to every attempt to appropriate public moneys — federal, state, or local — directly or indirectly, for the support of sectarian or private institutions."[8] As a sitting justice on the Supreme Court, Black's letters to Hill, Rogers, and Andrews concerning proposed legislation were nothing less than a breach of judicial ethics.

On May 4, 1945, Rogers again testified before the Senate Education and Labor Committee on behalf of the Grand Commander of the Scottish Rite and himself. Rogers read the Grand Commander's statement contending that "sectarian schools would become, among the nonpublic schools, the principal beneficiaries of Federal aid. Such a status would ultimately destroy not only the free independent character of our public schools but would establish in our national life an interdependence of state and church." Rogers again asserted that aid to parochial schools violated the principles of Madison's "Memorial and Remonstrance," Jefferson's Act for Religious Freedom, and *Quick Bear*. Continuing his diatribe against religious education, Rogers even attempted to demonstrate that education in Catholic schools leads to criminal behavior.

On December 12, 1945, Congress decided to table the legislation but continued to work through the issues during 1946 and 1947. No legislation regarding federal aid to education was passed, however, until the enactment of the Elementary and Secondary Act of 1965. This law denied parochial schoolchildren full participation in the benefits afforded to public schoolchildren.

It is important to note that during the hearings on aid to parochial schools, no member of Congress or of the Senate Education and Labor panel ever suggested that federal subsidies to private schools were unconstitutional. Masonry's repeated appeals to

---

[8] *Scottish Rite News Bulletin*, No. 61 (April 5, 1945), 7.

Madison's "Memorial and Remonstrance" and Jefferson's Act for Religious Freedom were for naught. Instead, the historical record demonstrates the government's support for parochial education and the moral and religious precepts of Christianity as a whole. It appeared that in the near future the government was going to enact legislation that would provide federal aid to church schools. If it was going to prevail, Freemasonry needed a Masonic intervention.

Masonic Court-Packing

Beginning in his second term, President Roosevelt began to pack the Supreme Court with Masons. From 1937 to 1944, Roosevelt appointed nine justices, six of whom were Masons, and the other three espoused Masonic philosophy. From 1945 to 1953, Roosevelt's successor, President Harry S. Truman, another 33rd-degree Mason, appointed four justices, all Masons. Hence, of the thirteen appointments to the Supreme Court made by Masonic presidents over this period, ten were Freemasons. The next two appointments to the court, made by President Eisenhower, were also Masons.

Beginning with President Roosevelt's appointments in 1941 and through the first three years of President Nixon's term (1971), Freemasons dominated the Supreme Court. These years marked an era of revolutionary liberalism and anti-Christian sentiment. The Masonic dominance of the court was as follows: 1941-46, five to four; 1946-49, seven to two; 1949-55, eight to one; 1956-57, seven to two; 1957-58, six to three; 1958-62, seven to two; 1962-69, six to three; and 1969-71, five to four.

It is no surprise that four Masons who were appointed to the Supreme Court by Roosevelt or Truman spoke in favor of the court-packing plan. These men were Hugo L. Black, James F. Byrnes,

Sherman Minton, and Robert H. Jackson.[9] Justice Jackson even admitted that he and those who shared Roosevelt's viewpoint on the Constitution had succeeded in their efforts to shape democracy in America through the appointment of "forward-looking" justices.[10]

Freemasonry's aim was to bring establishment-clause cases to the high court so they could be adjudicated by justices who shared the same Masonic philosophy of Church-State separation. Masonry succeeded. Beginning with the *Everson* decision in 1947, and for the next quarter century, the Supreme Court focused on establishment-clause cases. With its newfound enthusiasm for such cases, the court systematically eroded the Christian underpinnings of American government. The Masonic-dominated court took the legal doctrine of *stare decisis* — which holds that a principle of law established by one judicial decision must be followed in another judicial decision — and threw it out the window.

Everson — Masonic Activism on the Bench

In *Everson v. Board of Education*, 1947, a New Jersey statute allowed a township to reimburse parents for money spent in transporting their children to all schools, including Catholic schools. Because the statute afforded benefits to all citizens attending private or public schools, the Supreme Court affirmed that the program was constitutionally permissible. However, Justice Hugo Black, writing the majority opinion, set forth the Masonic interpretation of the establishment clause thus: "The First Amendment has erected a wall between church and state. That wall must be kept high and impregnable. We could not approve the slightest breach."

---

[9] Justice Sherman Minton converted to the Catholic faith and left Freemasonry, January 8, 1946.

[10] *The Struggle for Judicial Supremacy*, xiv.

As mentioned above, neither Madison's "Memorial and Remonstrance" nor Jefferson's Act for Religious Freedom was ever addressed in either the Constitutional Convention or other debates in the House and Senate when the establishment clause was being crafted. Thomas Jefferson was in France when the First Amendment was discussed in Congress and adopted, and James Madison was not successful in having any of his proposed language on the clause adopted. Virginia was the last state to ratify the constitutional amendments, and members of the Virginia legislature declared that the establishment clause permitted the use of tax money for the support of religion or its preachers. In fact, Black's desire to strip the government's ability to support and protect any and all religions is *contradicted* by Madison's "Memorial and Remonstrance," the very document Black attempts to quote in his favor. In it, Madison writes, "A just government . . . will be best supported by protecting every citizen in the enjoyment of his Religion with the same equal hand which protects his person and his property."

Justice Jackson's dissenting opinion supported the majority's novel interpretation of the establishment clause (all seven Masons were unanimous on the First Amendment interpretation), but strongly held that the New Jersey statute supporting reimbursements for a child's transportation to parochial school was unconstitutional. Jackson, a 33rd-degree Mason, wrote in *Everson* that the state "may not spend funds to secure religion against skepticism" and that such expenditures amounted to a "reward for piety" and compensation "for adherence to a creed."

But in a separate dissenting opinion written by Justice Rutledge and joined by Justices Jackson, Burton, and Frankfurter, the court took the Masonic viewpoint on the establishment clause to a new level. Rutledge, also a Mason, argued that citizens who desire religious instruction mixed in with secular education should not be afforded the same constitutional protections as those who prefer secular education without any reference to a supreme being. "Like St. Paul's freedom," Rutledge wrote in *Everson v. Board of Education*, "religious liberty with a great price must be bought. And for those who exercise it most fully, by insisting upon religious education for their children mixed with secular, by terms of our Constitution the price is greater than for others." Hence Justice Rutledge granted constitutional protection for those who professed no religion at all at the expense of those who did, even though the Framers did not intend the establishment clause to patronize nonbelievers.

The majority and dissenting opinions in *Everson* advocate the protection of nonbelievers under the establishment clause. History shows that the intent of the establishment clause was to protect and support those who recognize a supreme being and believe they have a duty toward that being. In "Memorial and Remonstrance," Madison recognized that one's first allegiance is to God: "Before any man can be considered as a member of Civil Society, he must be considered as a subject of the Governor of the Universe." Madison was also vehemently opposed to Freemasonry. The arguments in *Everson* for the separation of Church and State, first advanced by Scottish Rite Freemasonry and finally adopted by Masonic justices, became the law of the land. Those who professed no belief in God, a group viewed by the Framers with disapproval, gained newly minted rights under the U.S. Constitution.

Everson's Masonic Progeny

Since *Everson*, the wall of separation between Church and State has grown dramatically. In *McCollum v. Board of Education* (1948), a case taken up by the Supreme Court just a year after

Everson, the court declared unconstitutional an Illinois state law permitting released time for religious instruction in public schools, another ruling consistent with Scottish Rite Masonic philosophy. *McCollum* drew strong criticism from U.S. Catholic bishops, who said that this type of secularism is "the most deadly menace to our Christian and American way of living," and that establishing a policy of "indifference to religion" was an "utter distortion of history and law."[11]

The high court also struck down a Maryland state constitutional law requiring state officials to declare their belief in God (*Torcaso v. Watkins*, 1961); banned a New York Board of Regents recommendation that classes recite a prayer to "Almighty God" (*Engel v. Vitale*, 1962); declared unconstitutional a state law requiring that ten verses from the Bible be read aloud at the opening of each public school day (*Albington School District v. Schemp*, 1963); banned aid to colleges whose curriculums espoused religious teachings and exercises and whose clerics dominated the board of trustees (*Board of Public Works v. Horace Mann League*, 1966); held that a militant anti-church school group had standing to challenge the constitutionality of federal funding for sectarian schools (*Flast v. Cohen*, 1967); and prohibited public funding of salaries for parochial schoolteachers and state-funded instructional materials at such schools (*Lemon v. Kurtzman*, 1971).

The Supreme Court also proscribed public funding for maintenance and repair grants at parochial schools as well as tuition reimbursements and tax incentives for education at such schools (*Committee for Public Education v. Nyquist*, 1973); struck down a statute reimbursing parents for tuition paid to an elementary or secondary parochial school (*Sloan v. Lemon*, 1973); banned the

---

[11] *New York Times* (November 21, 1948).

reimbursement of parochial schools for their expenses in administering state-required and teacher-prepared tests (*Leavitt v. Committee for Public Education*, 1973); declared unconstitutional a statute allowing the lending of instructional materials and equipment to parochial schools (*Meek v. Pittenger*, 1975; *Wolman v. Walter*, 1977); struck down a statute that authorized posting the Ten Commandments on the walls of public school classrooms because there was "no secular legislative purpose" (*Stone v. Graham*, 1980); prohibited that community education classes be provided by public schoolteachers to parochial school students (*Aguilar v. Felton*, 1985; *Grand Rapids School District v. Ball*, 1985); and held unconstitutional a statute authorizing schools to set aside one minute at the start of the school day for meditation or voluntary prayer (*Wallace v. Jaffree*, 1985). With the eradication of Judeo-Christian principles that once guided our country, the court has subsequently redefined the meaning of obscenity and allowed the proliferation of salacious and depraved materials throughout our society.[12] This has caused irreparable damage to our country. All this has been done in the name of Masonic "Liberty, Equality, and Fraternity."

How has Masonry been able to achieve its objectives of de-Christianizing American schools and bringing about a separation of Church and State? Normally, the first step is to round up some taxpayers who will let their names be used in court cases. The Craft did find such taxpayers and other organizations, which it financed. Such groups included Protestants and Other Americans United for Separation of Church and State (now known as

---

[12] See, for example, *Roth v. United States*, 354 U.S. 476 (1957); *Kingsley Books v. Brown*, 354 U.S. 436 (1957); *Butler v. Michigan*, 352 U.S. 380 (1957); *Smith v. California*, 361 U.S. 147 (1959); *Manual Enterprises v. Day*, 370 U.S. 478 (1960); and *John Cleland's Memoirs of a Woman of Pleasure v. Attorney General*, 383 U.S. 413 (1966).

the Americans United, or the AU), the Horace Mann League, and PEARL (a New York State anti-church-school coalition).

The Scottish Rite Supreme Council also established a Committee on Education and Americanism. The *New Age* for January 1976 carried a report on the committee's recommendations. Masons and their families were urged to join organizations such as the AU and Americans for Public Schools in order to oppose aid to parochial schools; to educate each Master Mason on the importance of the separation of Church and State; to elect legislators opposed to government aid to parochial schools; to encourage men and women to frustrate the efforts of private schools to obtain government aid; to encourage those in the legal profession to monitor legislation and other legal activity regarding the establishment clause; and to distribute Masonic propaganda "through public and private schools and libraries." Freemasonry boasts that it has "provided the major obstacle" to the growth of religious education in America.[13]

The Scottish Rite Supreme Council, along with Masonic presidents, congressmen, and Supreme Court justices have played the most significant part in the secularization of our country. The *New Age* published: "The action of judges who were Masons in defending the liberties of the people from the encroachment of a power-hungry despot, oligarchy, bureaucracy [referring to the Catholic Church] . . . has been uniformly commendable."[14] The Scottish Rite Supreme Council, in explaining how Masonry has been able to empower their special-interest groups to bring these cases before Masonic justices, proudly proclaimed: "It can be done; it has been done."[15]

---

[13] *New Age,* William A. Brandenburg, *More than Ritual* (January 1959), 23, 26.

[14] Ibid., 25.

[15] *New Age,* Report of the Committee on Education and Americanism (January 1976), 19-22.

The Opposition by the Church

Pope Leo XIII recognized the motives of Masonry regarding the education of children long before they manifested themselves on American soil. In 1884, in his encyclical *Humanum Genus,* Leo wrote that

> the sect of the Freemasons also endeavors to take to itself the education of youth. They think that they can easily mold to their opinions that soft and pliant age, and bend it whither they will . . . and in many places they have procured that the education of youth shall be exclusively in the hands of laymen, and that nothing which treats of the most important and most holy duties of men to God shall be introduced into the instructions on morals. (No. 21)

Pope Leo recognized Freemasonry's fanatical desire to control public education was to indoctrinate the youth into relativism, so that "each one must be left at liberty to follow, when he becomes of age, whatever he may prefer." Leo called such a view of religion "a rashness unknown to the very pagans" (No. 21).

Just as other popes had warned about the Lodge's teaching of indifferentism, Leo likewise warned in *Humanum Genus* that Masonry's removal of Christian education from public schools would result in a degradation of morality:

> For, wherever, by removing Christian education, this teaching has begun more completely to rule, there goodness and integrity of morals have begun quickly to perish, monstrous and shameful opinions have grown up, and the audacity of evil deeds has risen to a high degree. (No. 19)

Similarly, in his encyclical *Immortale Dei*, issued in 1885, Leo wrote:

Human societies cannot, without becoming criminal, act as if God did not exist or refuse to concern themselves with religion, as though it were something foreign to them, or of no purpose to them. . . . As for the Church, which has God Himself for its author, to exclude her from the active life of the nation, from the laws, the education of the young, the family, is to commit a great and pernicious error. (Nos. 6, 32)

Pope Leo also stated that the Church-State separation advocated by Masonry was an attack on the Church's teaching authority:

By a long and persevering labor, they endeavor to bring about this result — namely, that the teaching office and authority of the Church may become of no account in the civil State; and for this same reason they declare to the people and contend that the Church and State ought to be altogether disunited. (No. 13)

In his 1887 encyclical letter *Officio Sanctissimo*, Pope Leo declared that "it is wrong for civil power to take umbrage at and to be offended by the Church's liberty, since the source of civil power and of religious power is one and the same; namely God. That is why there can never be between them either disagreement, or mutual obstruction, or interference, since God cannot be at variance with Himself and there can never be any conflict in His works" (No. 13).

Blessed Pius IX similarly identified the errors that flow from removing religion from the civil society. In his 1864 encyclical *Quanta Cura*, he wrote that "where religion has been removed from civil society, and the doctrine and authority of divine revelation repudiated, the genuine notion itself of justice and human right is darkened and lost" (No. 4). The Scottish Rite called the

Pope's encyclical "the most dogmatic attack on freedom ever penned by a human being."[16]

In his encyclical on liberalism and religious indifferentism, Pope Gregory XVI also denounced "the plans of those who desire vehemently to separate the Church from the state," calling it certain "that the concord which always was favorable and beneficial for the sacred and the civil order is feared by the shameless lovers of liberty."[17] In what one hopes is not a prophecy of America's fate, Pope Gregory said, in 1832: "Experience shows, even from earliest times, that cities renowned for wealth, dominion, and glory perished as a result of this single evil, namely immoderate freedom of opinion, license of free speech, and desire for novelty."[18]

In *Vehementer Nos* (1906), St. Pius X likewise rejected the notion of a radical separation of Church and State as "absolutely false," and a "most pernicious error" that injures society itself "for it cannot either prosper or last long when due place is not left for religion, which is the Supreme rule and the sovereign mistress in all questions touching the rights and duties of men" (No. 3). This rejection was explicitly reiterated by Pius XI in *Maximam Gravissimamque* in 1924 (No. 2).

Freemasonry and the New World Order

There is much speculation in our society about the coming of a New World Order. This New World Order is generally identified with two movements — one toward a one-world government; the other toward a one-world religion. Some believe that Freemasonry, with its secret religious teachings and its powerful influence in all

---

[16] *New Age* (February 1959), 71-72.

[17] *Mirari Vos* (August 15, 1832), No. 20.

[18] Ibid., No. 14.

three branches of government (executive, legislative, and judicial), is the vehicle by which the New World Order will be realized.

Freemasonry has not been bashful about its goal of achieving a New World Order governed by Masonic principles. The *New Age* has said that Freemasonry is "the missionary of the new order — a Liberal order."[19] Indeed, Masonry views the success of its establishment-clause cases as ushering in this new societal order, one devoid of Christ and his Church. Masonry's popular authors have also celebrated the new order that the Craft is working to bring about. Masonry, according to H. L. Haywood, "is a world law, destined to change the earth into conformity with itself, and as a world power it is something superb, awe-inspiring, godlike."[20] In 1951, Joseph Fort Newton wrote that Freemasonry's aim was "to bring about a universal league of mankind" and "to form mankind into a great redemptive brotherhood."[21] In the 32nd degree of the Scottish Rite of Freemasonry, the candidate is told that "Masonry will eventually rule the world," and the brethren are to pray for the "universal dominion of the true principles of Masonry."

The separation of Church and State, brought about largely by Freemasonry, is evidence that Masonry is succeeding in its effort to bring about a New World Order of secularism. Organizations such as the World Constitution and Parliament Association, the Council on Foreign Relations, the United Nations, the Trilateral Commission, NATO, the World Council of Churches, the World Future Society and other worldwide organizations seeking unification of power and ideology are viewed by some as having Masonic undertones.

Many are also suspicious of our government's continued role in the Masonic movement. We have already examined Masonry's

---

[19] *New Age*, Dr. James D. Carter, *Why Stand Ye Here Idle?* (March 1959), 155.

[20] *The Great Teachings of Masonry*, 90.

[21] *The Builders: A Story and Study of Freemasonry*, 233.

influence on the Supreme Court. In addition, seventeen U.S. presidents have been Master Masons, and Congress has always had a considerable Masonic influence, although this influence has declined in recent years.[22] The Great Seal of our country — which was adopted by the Continental Congress in 1782 and made its appearance on the reverse side of the one-dollar bill during the administration of Franklin Roosevelt (a 33rd-degree Mason) — includes Masonic symbolism and wording. This seal features the Masonic All-Seeing Eye and bears the inscription *Novus Ordo Seclorum* ("New Order of the Ages," or "New World Order").

We should not exaggerate Freemasonry's power. At the same time, however, we must bear in mind that Masonry, with its secularizing agenda and religious indifferentism, is, in the words of Pope Leo XIII, "the implacable enemy of Christ and of the Church."[23] We must pray daily for its defeat.

---

[22] Congressional Masonic membership has declined from about seventy percent in the 1920s to fifty percent in the 1950s, to about fifteen percent currently. The statistics, of course, are based on the person's willingness to disclose Masonic affiliation.

[23] Encyclical, *Custodi di Quella Fede*, (December 8, 1892), No. 6.

Chapter

IX

WHY WOULD A CHRISTIAN REMAIN IN THE LODGE?

We have seen how men are enticed into joining Freemasonry. We have also considered how Christians can be deceived into believing that the Lodge is a Christian institution. But why would an informed Christian remain in the Lodge?

Some Christians remain because of invincible ignorance. Most Masons, after initiation, do not regularly participate in Lodge activities. Many join the Blue lodge only because they want to become Shriners. A lodge may have two hundred or three hundred members, but in many cases only the eleven or twelve officers and a few other brothers show up for meetings or degree presentations. Most Masonic rituals are esoteric and cannot be fully understood without extensive study. Typically, only lodge officers who do the degree work have access to their jurisdiction's code of ritual. Moreover, usually only one or two Masons in a particular lodge are responsible for performing the lengthy portions of Masonic ritual. Hence, knowledge of Masonic ritual among the brethren is generally very limited.

Masonry's own authorities acknowledge the ignorance of most Masons. Allen Roberts says that there "is much that is still unknown even to the ardent Masonic student."[1] Masonic writer Rollin Blackmer says, "It is a lamentable fact that the great mass of our membership are . . . densely ignorant with everything connected with Masonry."[2] An official text from the Grand Lodge of Georgia says: "The majority of Masons are sadly lacking in the knowledge of the height, breadth and depth of Masonic teachings as contained in the meanings of the many symbols of Masonry."[3] Edmond Ronayne points out the irony that "those who know the least about Freemasonry are the Masons themselves."[4]

This is often why Masons do not try to defend Masonic rituals when they are challenged about the incompatibility of Masonry and Christianity. Because they love their organization but are unfamiliar with its rituals, they can become quite defensive when confronted. They often resort to attacking the anti-Masonic messenger, and not the message. This is called an *ad hominem* argument: a person attacks an opponent's character instead of answering his contentions. Because most of the information concerning Masonry comes from men who have left the Lodge, Masons are likely to question the credibility of those former Masons on the ground that they have violated their Masonic obligations — even though many of the rituals can be found in the public domain. Masons also have to contend with the fact that thousands of Christian men who have left the Lodge give the same reasons for leaving: indifference toward Christ and improper oaths. Christian Masons have nowhere to appeal but their own authorities. Of the hundreds of books written by Freemasons, there is not a single book that provides a Christian defense of the Lodge against the problems of indifferentism, syncretism, and false swearing.

---

[1] *The Craft and its Symbols*, 6.
[2] *The Lodge and the Craft*, 1.
[3] *Leaves from Georgia Masonry*, Grand Lodge of Georgia (1947), 65.
[4] *The Master's Carpet or Masonry and Baal Worship — Identical*, 242.

Many Christians remain in the Lodge even though they acknowledge the incongruity between their faith and some of the Lodge's teachings. They rationalize that the positives outweigh the negatives. After all, Freemasonry has enabled them to form wonderful friendships with other Masons and their families. The Masonic lodge serves as a support system for members who endure such hardships as the loss of a job or a death in the family. Through their lodges, Masons participate in charitable activities for the community. Masons therefore question how their organization, which does so much good, can be criticized by Christians, who are supposed to love their neighbors as themselves.

But the good things of the Lodge are not the focus. It is the religious teachings of Freemasonry that are chiefly at issue. The men of the Lodge, in many cases, are moral and righteous. The question that the Christian Mason must ask himself, however, is whether or not Masonry's teachings about God and eternal life are true. This judgment must be based upon the teachings of the Lodge, not on the conduct of its members.

Masonic oaths and secrecy also keep Christian men in Masonry even when their membership in the Lodge causes them tremendous religious tension. Stephen Knight, who has interviewed hundreds of Masons in his study of Freemasonry, reports: "It has been said that these issues are of no concern to Freemasons, but hundreds of members of the Brotherhood have spoken to me of the turmoil they experience in attempting to reconcile their religious views with the demands of Masonic ritual."[5]

A Mason may adjust his attitude toward the institution's rituals that he feels may be at odds with his preexisting religious beliefs. Instead, he focuses on how many presidents were Masons

---

[5] *The Brotherhood: The Explosive Exposé of the Secret World of the Freemasons*, 231.

or how much good Masonry does for the community. This change in attitude is less costly, psychologically speaking, than leaving Masonry or speaking out against the Craft. It may even lead the Christian Mason to defend Freemasonry in spite of the disharmony he feels. Psychologists call this process of changing one's attitude toward something that causes internal disharmony "cognitive dissonance." This also explains why the general public has little understanding about what goes on behind the lodge doors.

Many Masons also fear the ramifications of violating the oaths they have sworn to God. The Mason takes seriously the warning that breaking his vow defiles his living temple and "imposes not hours but ages of misery."[6] They also hear about the "Morgan Affair." William Morgan was a captain in the War of 1812 who wrote an exposé on Freemasonry. Masons are said to have kidnapped him, and he was never seen alive again. His body was later discovered, and three men were given prison terms for their part in the affair. A monument in Batavia, New York, has been erected to his memory, which reads: "Sacred to the memory of Wm. Morgan, a native of Virginia, a captain in the War of 1812, a respectable citizen of Batavia and a martyr to the freedom of writing, printing and speaking the truth. He was abducted from near this spot in the year 1826, by Freemasons, and murdered for revealing the secrets of their order."[7]

Martin Wagner makes this observation in his extensive study of Freemasonry:

> That Masons believe that these penalties will be mercilessly inflicted upon them, should they betray its secrets, we know to be true in many cases. The convictions of those who have

---

[6] Hall, *The Lost Keys of Freemasonry or the Secret of Hiram Abiff*, 68.
[7] See, for example, Whalen, *Christianity and American Freemasonry*, 19-20.

exposed the ritualism of the order, that they took their lives into their hands in doing so is proof. The numerous confessions made to the writer, on the part of both Masons and ex-Masons, is further proof.[8]

Another reason men remain in the Lodge is pride. Many in Masonry receive prestige and respect that they cannot find outside of the Lodge. In Freemasonry, individuals enjoy important titles, don fancy regalia, and hold positions of authority. These vices can be difficult to overcome for those with a strong desire to feel important and be accepted. Further, out of fear of losing friendships or being perceived as judgmental, these men cannot even imagine abandoning their lodge brothers. These traps blind Christians from the reality of the Lodge, and lead them to love the praise of men more than the praise of God (cf. Jn 12:43). The Lord warns us: "What does it profit a man, to gain the whole world and forfeit his life?" (Mk 8:36).

A Mason's pride can cloud his desire to want to know the truth. If God is really important to the Christian Mason who is presented with the Christian arguments against the Lodge, he must take these arguments seriously. He must humble himself and ask the Lord for the grace to discern the truth. The Lord promises that those who humble themselves will be exalted (cf. Mt 23:12; Lk 14:11; 18:14). If he refuses even to try to discern what is true and good, his continued participation in Freemasonry is no longer innocent (cf. CCC 1791). He is culpable for his actions. St. Peter warns us: "For if, after they have escaped the defilements of the world through the knowledge of our Lord and Savior Jesus Christ, they are again entangled in them and overpowered, the last state has become worse for them than the first. For it would have been better for them never to have known the way of righteousness than

---

[8] *Freemasonry: An Interpretation*, 550.

after knowing it to turn back from the holy commandment delivered to them" (2 Pet 2:20-21).

Many Christian Masons know that if they address the teachings of the Lodge head on, they will have to change their lives radically. They are afraid that if they ask, they will receive (cf. Mt 7:7). They fear conversion. It is easier for some to ignore the issues and remain in darkness. Instead, they presume upon the riches of God's patience and kindness. But St. Paul teaches us that God's patience is meant *to lead us to repentance* (cf. Rom 2:4). If we refuse to repent, then God will refuse us (cf. 2 Tim 2:12).

Christian Masons must decide whether they really believe in the objective truth of Jesus Christ, and whether to conform their lives to reflect that belief. Then they will choose either to enter "through the narrow gate" of Jesus Christ or the wider gate of Freemasonry (cf. Mt 7:13-14). Jesus has told us there is only one way (cf. Jn 14:6): "I am the light of the world; he who follows me will not walk in darkness, but will have the light of life" (Jn 8:12).

Amen.

We tore from the face of masonry the mask
which it used to hide itself and We showed it
in its crude deformity and dark fatal activity.

— POPE LEO XIII

Appendix

A

LETTER OF RESIGNATION

A Mason must inform his mother Blue lodge that he wishes to resign from the Craft. Because the Blue lodge is the foundation of Freemasonry, resigning from it automatically terminates one's membership in any other Masonic organizations, such as the Scottish Rite, the York Rite, or the Shriners.

The resignation should be done by letter. If the letter is addressed to the members of a particular lodge, most jurisdictions require the Secretary to read the letter aloud in open lodge to all who are present. This provides an excellent opportunity for a former Mason to educate the membership about the truth of Jesus Christ and the incompatibility of Freemasonry with Christianity. Such a letter of resignation may plant a seed in the hearts of other men who are privately seeking the truth. It also creates a record and resolves questions that may exist or arise concerning the resignation.

The following is a sample letter of resignation:

Members of _____ Lodge No. ____:

This is to inform you of my resignation from Freemasonry. I can no longer be a Mason because I now see that the teachings of the Lodge are incompatible with the Christian faith.

Through its rituals and symbolism, Freemasonry promotes the error of indifferentism, the belief that all religions are equally legitimate paths to God. While Masonry teaches about the Great Architect of the Universe, it is silent about the Incarnation. While Masonry teaches that purity of life and conduct are necessary to gain admission to the celestial lodge above, it is silent about our sinfulness and the need for the Redeemer. While Masonry teaches about the resurrection of the body in the Hiramic Legend, it is silent about Jesus Christ. The Lodge gives its members the impression that these truths of Christian faith are optional, not essential, to our salvation.

Freemasonry also treats the Holy Bible as a symbol of God's will, rather than the revealed written word of God. Masonry thus views Christianity as parallel or complementary to other religious traditions, not superior to them. Consequently, the Lodge welcomes any other religious writing to take an equal place with the Bible on the Masonic altar. All truths are made relative for the greater glory of Masonic fellowship.

As a Christian, I believe that God, out of his eternal love for humanity, has chosen to reveal himself completely and definitively in the Person of Jesus Christ, who declared, "I am the way, and the truth, and the life; no one comes to the Father but by me" (Jn 14:6). God also wants all people to come to the knowledge of this truth. Because God is infinite love and eternal truth, he cannot be pleased with Freemasonry's treatment of his revelation as optional. He cannot be indifferent to what a man believes. Otherwise, both truth and falsehood would be consonant with his nature. This denies who God is.

Freemasonry should be commended for doing many charitable works for the common good and fostering wonderful and lasting friendships among its members. But these things cannot be put above the fullness of God's revealed truth. Charity, brotherly love, and ultimately our eternal destiny must be founded on truth. While Freemasonry claims to be an organization in search of truth, one must ask what good its search is if the truth is never found. For the Lodge, the definition of truth is left to the subjective whim of each member. For the Christian, the fullness of truth is found in his only-begotten Son, the Lord Jesus Christ.

In Christ,

_____

Former Mason

Appendix

B

GLOSSARY OF MASONIC TERMS

Acacia — The Masonic symbol of the immortality of the soul and resurrection to new life.

All-Seeing Eye — A Masonic symbol for the supreme deity.

Altar — The most important article of furniture in a lodge room. On it rest the Volume of the Sacred Law, Square, and Compasses.

Anchor and Ark — Emblems of a well-grounded hope and a well-spent life.

Anno Lucis — "Year of Light." The Masonic parallel to the Christian *Anno Domini*. (Since Masonry holds that creation took place four thousand years before Christ, the year 2006 would be Masonically represented as *Anno Lucis* 6006.)

Apron — The required attire for any formal Masonic assembly. Worn around the waist, called "the badge of a Mason," the apron represents the purity of life and conduct necessary to gain admission into heaven.

Ashlar — The Perfect Ashlar is a hewn, or squared, stone. It symbolizes the state of perfection at which a Mason hopes to arrive. The Rough Ashlar is a symbol of a Mason's rude and imperfect state by nature.

Beehive — An emblem of industry. It teaches Masons that, as intelligent beings, they should be ever industrious.

Blazing Star — The Masonic symbol of divine providence.

Blue Lodge — The body of Freemasonry that confers the degrees of Entered Apprentice, Fellowcraft, and Master Mason. It may also refer to a particular lodge under the jurisdiction of a Grand Lodge.

Boaz — The secret name for the grip of an Entered Apprentice. It denotes strength and is only given in a secret, syllabic exchange between two Masons. It is also the name of the left brazen pillar of King Solomon's Temple.

Book of Constitutions — The book that reminds Masons to be guarded in their thoughts, words, and actions, particularly in the presence of Masonry's enemies, bearing in mind the Masonic virtues of silence and circumspection.

Cabletow — The rope that a candidate wears during his initiation into the three degrees. In the Entered Apprentice degree, the cabletow, worn around the candidate's neck, symbolizes his tie to the profane world. In the Fellowcraft and Master Mason degrees, it is worn around the arm and waist, respectively, to symbolize the Mason's tie to the Lodge.

Celestial Lodge Above — Masonry's name for heaven.

Chalk — Symbol of the freedom with which operative Entered Apprentices served their Masters. Its slightest touch leaves a trace behind.

Charcoal — Symbol of the fervency with which operative Entered Apprentices served their Masters. Well-ignited charcoal causes the most obdurate metals to yield.

Circumambulation — The process of conducting a blindfolded candidate around the lodge room as he is examined by the principal officers.

Clandestine — An irregular Mason. One who has not yet been accepted under the authority of a recognized Grand Lodge.

Clay — Symbol of the zeal with which operative Entered Apprentices served their Masters. Clay also represents the earth, reminding the brethren that from it we came, and to it we must all return.

Coffin — That which received the remains of Hiram Abif. A reminder of death.

Common Gavel — In Operative Masonry, the tool used to break off the corners of rough stones. In Speculative Masonry, a symbol of the Mason's effort to divest his mind and conscience of the vices and superfluities of life in order to become fit for heaven.

Cowan — One who attempts to procure the secrets of Freemasonry unlawfully by eavesdropping or pretending to be a Mason.

Craft Masonry — Another name for Blue Lodge Masonry, the authority that confers the three degrees.

Degree — The ceremony or ritual in which a candidate receives a particular level of Masonic status.

Demit — The process of terminating a man's membership in a Masonic lodge. Also the document evidencing the termination.

Discalceation — The rite in which a candidate for a Masonic degree removes his shoes and is invested with special slippers before being admitted into the lodge.

Divestiture — The rite in which a candidate for a Masonic degree removes his outer clothing worn in the profane world before being admitted into the lodge.

Due Guard — The secret sign simulating the position in which a candidate's hands were placed on the Volume of the Sacred Law while swearing his Masonic oath.

Entered Apprentice — One who has completed the first degree of Blue Lodge Masonry.

Fellowcraft — One who has completed the second degree of Blue Lodge Masonry.

Five Points of Fellowship — The position to which the Master Mason is raised in the third degree and receives the Grand Masonic Word: foot to foot, knee to knee, breast to breast, hand to back, and cheek to cheek or mouth to ear.

Five Senses — Hearing, seeing, feeling, smelling, and tasting, the first three of which are most important in Masonry. A Mason hears the word, sees the sign, and feels the grip by which Masons may know one another.

Furniture of the Lodge — The Volume of the Sacred Law, the Square, the Compasses, and the Masonic altar.

The Letter *G* — The most common Masonic symbol for God in English-speaking countries. The letter *G* stands for God, Geometry, and Gnosis.

GAOTU — Acronym for Masonry's name for God, the Great (or Grand) Architect of the Universe.

Grand Hailing Sign of Distress — The secret sign given by a Master Mason when he is in danger.

Grand Lodge — The supreme governing body of Freemasonry in a given jurisdiction. There are fifty-one Grand Lodges in the United States.

Grand Masonic Word — The secret word *Ma-Ha-Bone*. It is always given between two Masons on the Five Points of Fellowship, in syllabic form and in low breath.

Great Lights — The Volume of the Sacred Law, the Square, and Compasses. The Great Lights are displayed during open lodge.

Grips — Secret handshakes of the various degrees.

Hiram Abif — In Masonic legend, the master builder of King Solomon's Temple. The savior of Freemasonry.

Hiramic Legend — The death-burial-and-resurrection rite of the third degree of Blue Lodge Masonry.

Hoodwink — The blindfold used during a candidate's initiation into Masonic degrees.

Hourglass — An emblem of the brevity of human life.

Jabulon — Masonry's secret name for God, revealed in the Royal Arch degree of the York Rite.

Jachin — Secret name for the grip of a Fellowcraft. It denotes establishment and is always given in a secret, syllabic exchange between two Masons. It is also the name of the right brazen pillar of King Solomon's Temple.

Jewels — Each lodge has six jewels, three immovable and three movable. The three immovable jewels are the Square, which teaches morality; the Level, which teaches equality; and the Plumb, which teaches rectitude of conduct. The three movable jewels are the Rough Ashlar, the Perfect Ashlar, and the Trestleboard.

Labor — The Lodge at work, either conducting a business meeting or conferring a degree.

Landmarks — The most fundamental and unalterable tenets of Freemasonry. While there is no universal agreement on the Landmarks, most versions include belief in God, immortality, resurrection, symbolism, secrecy, modes of recognition, and physical qualifications of candidates.

Lesser Lights — The three burning lights situated near the altar. They represent the sun, the moon, and the Master of the Lodge.

Level — In Operative Masonry, a tool used to prove horizontals. In Speculative Masonry, a symbol of equality.

Lost Word — Refers to divine knowledge, or the name of deity. In the Hiramic Legend, the Fellowcrafts murdered Hiram Abif because he would not disclose the Lost Word.

Ma-Ha-Bone — The Grand Masonic word, uttered in syllabic form and low breath to the newly raised Master Mason on the Five Points of Fellowship.

Master Mason — One who has completed the third, and highest, degree of Blue Lodge Masonry.

Northeast Corner — In Operative Masonry, the place where Masons usually laid the first stone. In Speculative Masonry, the part of the lodge where the newly initiated Entered Apprentice receives his first instruction.

Obligations — Masonic oaths sworn by the candidate as part of his initiation.

Officers of the Lodge — Worshipful Master, Senior and Junior Wardens, Senior and Junior Deacons, Senior and Junior Stewards, Tiler, Secretary, Treasurer (or Secretary-Treasurer), Lodge Counselor, and Chaplain. May also include Marshal, Organist, or Soloist.

Operative Masonry — A term indicating the building of physical structures. Also, the ancient guild members who built Europe's great cathedrals during the Middle Ages.

Ornaments of the Lodge — The Mosaic Pavement (symbolic of good and evil), Indented Tessel (symbolic of blessings and comforts), and Blazing Star (symbolic of divine providence). The Mosaic Pavement and Indented Tessel also represent the ground floor of King Solomon's Temple.

Pass — Password. There are two passes in Blue Lodge Masonry: *Shibboleth* (Fellowcraft degree) and *Tubal-Cain* (Master Mason degree).

Petition — The formal application a candidate submits to the lodge to request a Masonic degree.

Plumb — In Operative Masonry, a device used to raise perpendiculars. In Speculative Masonry, it is used to admonish the Mason to walk uprightly before God and man.

Pot of Incense — Symbol of a pure heart, which is always an acceptable sacrifice to deity.

Profane — One who has not been initiated into the degrees of Freemasonry: a non-Mason.

Proficiency Man — One who has been formally recognized by his Grand Lodge as an expert in performing Masonic ritual and is authorized to give instruction in Masonic ritual.

Refreshment — Term used to describe the lodge at momentary rest (the lodge is called "from labor to refreshment").

Regular — That which is universally recognized by Freemasonry.

Scythe — An emblem of time, which cuts the thread of life and launches Masons into eternity.

Setting Maul — In Masonic legend, the mallet used to murder Hiram Abif. An emblem of those casualties and diseases by which our earthly existence may be terminated.

Seven Liberal Arts and Sciences — Grammar, rhetoric, logic, arithmetic, geometry, music, and astronomy. Most revered among Masons is geometry because it is said to offer the surest proof of God's existence.

Shibboleth — The secret password of the Fellowcraft degree. It also refers to the secret pass grip of a Fellowcraft.

Shock of Enlightenment — The moment at which the hoodwink is removed from the Entered Apprentice after he has sworn the oath at the Masonic altar.

Signs — The secret gestures that simulate the self-mutilation and death penalties carried by the Masonic oaths.

Spade — The implement that dug the grave of Hiram Abif. A reminder of death.

Speculative Masonry — The teaching of moral and religious truths using operative stonemasons' tools and terminology to build a man's spiritual temple (soul).

Square — One of the Great Lights of Masonry. It is a tool used in Operative Masonry to square off the work. In Speculative Masonry, it symbolizes morality.

Sword Pointing to Naked Heart — Symbol of justice and the knowledge that God will reward all good Masons according to their merits.

Symbolic Lodge — Same as Blue lodge.

Three Great Pillars — The three symbolic supports of the Lodge, representing wisdom, strength, and beauty.

Three Steps — Symbols of the three principal stages of a man's life: youth, manhood, and age. The steps also represent the three Masonic degrees (Entered Apprentice, Fellowcraft, and Master Mason), as well as the three principal officers of the Lodge (Junior Warden, Senior Warden, and Worshipful Master).

Tiler (or Tyler) — The Mason who guards the outer door of the lodge in order to determine that those who enter are regular Masons.

Token of the Pass — The secret handshake that coincides with the pass.

Trestleboard — Symbol of the tracing board on which a Mason erects his spiritual and moral designs.

Trowel — In Operative Masonry, a tool used to spread cement. In Speculative Masonry, it is symbolically used to spread the cement of love and affection, thus uniting all Masons into one sacred band of friends and brothers.

Tubal-Cain — The secret name of the pass grip of a Master Mason. Also refers to the eighth man from Adam, who, having perfected himself in masonry, is also the first known maker of bronze and iron tools.

Twenty-Four-Inch Gauge — Tool used in Operative Masonry to measure and lay out the work. In Speculative Masonry, it divides a Mason's time into a twenty-four-hour day with three equal parts: eight hours for the service of God and relief of distressed worthy brothers, eight hours for usual vocations, and eight hours for refreshment and sleep.

Volume of the Sacred Law — Any book placed on the Masonic altar that symbolizes God's will. In the United States, this book is typically the Holy Bible, but it can be accompanied by other religious writings.

Winding Staircase — Symbol of a Mason's spiritual and moral advancement by means of the Masonic degrees (three steps), human senses (five steps), and the liberal arts (seven steps).

Words — The secret names for the various grips in Freemasonry.

Working Tools — Implements of Operative Masonry that are used to teach moral and spiritual truths to the Speculative Mason. These include the Common Gavel, Square, Level, Plumb, and Trowel.

Worshipful Master — The highest officer of a Masonic lodge.

MASONIC LANDMARKS

(Please note that the following Masonic Landmarks are reprinted here as they were originally written.)

Dr. Albert Mackey's Landmarks

1. The modes of recognition.
2. The division of symbolic Masonry into three degrees.
3. The legend of the third degree.
4. The government of the Freemasonry by a Grand Master.
5. The prerogative of the Grand Master to preside over every assembly of the Craft.
6. The prerogative of the Grand Master to grant dispensations for conferring degrees at irregular intervals.
7. The prerogative of the Grand Master to give dispensations for opening and holding Lodges.
8. The prerogative of the Grand Master to make Masons at sight.
9. The necessity for Masons to congregate in Lodges.
10. The government of the Craft, when so congregated in a Lodge, by a Master and two Wardens.
11. The necessity that every Lodge, when congregated, should be duly tiled.

12. The right of every Mason to be represented in all general meetings of the Craft.

13. The right of every Mason to appeal from the decision of his brethren, in Lodge convened, to the Grand Master.

14. The right of every Mason to visit and sit in every regular Lodge.

15. That no visitor, unknown to the brethren present or to someone of them as a Mason, can enter a Lodge without first passing an examination according to ancient usage.

16 No Lodge can interfere with the business of another Lodge.

17. Every Freemason is amenable to the laws and regulations of the Masonic jurisdiction in which he resides.

18. A candidate for initiation must be a man unmutilated, free born and of mature age.

19. A belief in the existence of God as the Grand Architect of the Universe.

20. Belief in a resurrection to a future life.

21. A "Book of the Law" constitutes an indispensable part of the furniture of every Lodge.

22. The equality of all Masons.

23. The secrecy of the Institution.

24. The foundation of speculative science upon an operative art, and the symbolic use of terms of that are for the purpose of moral teaching.

25. These Landmarks can never be changed.

Luke Lockwood's Landmarks

1. Belief in the existence of a Supreme Being, in some revelation of His will, in the Resurrection of the Body and in the Immortality of the Soul.

2. The obligations and modes of recognition and the Legend of the Third Degree.

3. The inculcation of the moral virtues, of benevolence and of the doctrines of Natural Religion, by means of symbols derived from the Temple of King Solomon and its tradition, and from usages and customs observed, and from the implements and materials used in its construction.

4. That Masons must obey the moral law and the government of the country in which they live.

5. That the Grand Master is the Head of the Craft.

6. That the Master is the Head of the Lodge.

7. That the Grand Lodge is the Supreme Governing Body within its territorial jurisdiction.

8. That every Lodge has an inherent right to be represented in Grand Lodge by its first three officers or their proxies.

9. That every Lodge has power to make Masons, and to administer its own private affairs.

10. That every candidate must be a man, of lawful age, born of free parents, under no restraint of liberty, and hale and sound as a man ought to be.

11. That no candidate can be received except by unanimous ballot, after due notice of his application and due inquiry as to his qualifications.

12. That the ballot is inviolably secret.

13. That all Masons, as such, are peers.

14. That all Lodges are peers.

15. That all Grand Lodges are peers.

16. That no person can be installed Master of a Lodge unless he be a Past Warden, except by dispensation of the Grand Master.

17. That the obligations, means of recognition, and the forms and ceremonies observed in conferring degrees are secret.

18. That no innovation can be made upon the body of Masonry.

19. That the Ancient Landmarks are the Supreme Law, and cannot be changed or abrogated.

H. B. Grant's Landmarks

1. The Ancient Landmarks of Freemasonry are the immemorial usages and fundamental principles of the Craft, and are unchangeable.
2. Anciently, Freemasonry was both operative and speculative; it is now speculative, embracing a system of ethics, moral, religious and philosophical and relates to the social, ethical and intellectual progress of man.
3. Freemasonry embraces the degrees of Entered Apprentice, Fellow Craft and Master Mason, conferred in regular Lodges whose rites and ceremonies are private.
4. The legend of the third degree is a part of it.
5. Secrecy is an essential element of Freemasonry, and every Mason is bound by irrevocable ties to keep inviolate its private ceremonies, signs, words and business of the lodge and (except treason and murder) never to divulge any secret that may be confided by a brother if accepted as such.
6. Writing or printing the esoteric part of Freemasonry by word, syllable or signs, is contrary to the covenants of the fraternity.
7. The covenants of a Mason do not conflict with his duty to God, his country, his family, his neighbor, or himself, but are binding upon his conscience and actions.
8. Belief in the existence of, and reverencing the name of, the Supreme Being, whom men call God and whom Masons refer to as "The Grand Architect of the Universe," is unqualifiedly demanded.
9. Belief in the immortality of the soul and the resurrection to a future life.
10. "The Book of the Law," with the Square and Compasses, are the Great Lights in Freemasonry, and their presence in open lodge is indispensable.

11. The Great Tenets of Freemasonry are Brotherly Love, Relief and Truth.

12. The Cardinal Virtues of Freemasonry are Temperance, Fortitude, Prudence and Justice.

13. The white lambskin apron is the badge of a Mason.

14. The Square and Compasses are Masonic symbols of morality.

15. The Saints John's Days (June 24 and December 27) are Masonic Festival Days. One of which is the time for the annual election of officers.

16. The "General Assembly" or Grand Lodge, is the Supreme legislative, judicial and executive body of the Craft in all matters Masonic within its territorial jurisdiction, and is composed of representatives from lodges therein.

17. A lodge is a regularly organized body of Freemasons, having a Warrant of Constitution authorizing it to work in conformity with the laws and usages of the Craft.

18. Every Lodge, Grand or Subordinate, when lawfully congregated, must be regularly clothed, tiled and opened, before it can proceed to work.

19. Freemasons meet in the lodge upon the level of equality, and address each other as brother, when assembled.

20. A lodge, duly opened, has the right to instruct its representatives to Grand Lodge.

21. Questions of politics or sectarian religious belief cannot be brought into the lodge.

22. A Freemason in good fellowship with some regular Lodge of Freemasons, may visit any Lodge not his own when it will not disturb the harmony of the lodge visited.

23. A Freemason cannot sit in a clandestine lodge nor converse upon the secrets of Freemasonry with a clandestine Mason, nor with one who is under suspension or expulsion.

24. The Grand Master is the executive head of the Craft and the presiding officer of the Grand Lodge, by which he is elected, and whose laws he must obey.
25. The Grand Master may preside in any lodge in his jurisdiction.
26. The Grand Master may suspend the Master of a lodge or arrest a lodge charter for cause.
27. The officers of the lodge are the Master, the Senior Warden, Junior Warden, Treasurer, Secretary, Senior Deacon, Junior Deacon, Steward and Tiler.
28. The Master is the head of the lodge, and, as a presiding officer, governs it according to the laws and usages of the fraternity, and may convene it at pleasure.
29. The Master must have been a Warden (except in the formation of a new lodge, or when no Past Master or Past Warden, who is competent and willing to serve, is a member of the Lodge).
30. The Master, by virtue of his office, represents his lodge in Grand Lodge.
31. The Master of a lodge becomes "Past Master" at the close of his official term — (that is, has passed the chair into and out of it by serving his term).
32. The Wardens of a lodge must be Master Masons.
33. In the absence of the Master, the Senior Warden performs his duties. In the absence of both, the Junior Warden acts. If all are absent, the Junior Past Master of the lodge who is present and a member thereof, may preside at a stated or lawfully called meeting.
34. Officers of a lodge, Grand or Subordinate, hold their offices until their successors are lawfully chosen and inducted into office, or become lawfully disqualified.
35. A Mason is not to urge any person to become a candidate for the mysteries of Masonry, for every candidate must offer himself voluntarily and unsolicited.

36. Every candidate must be a man, free born, of mature and discreet age, of good morals and report, possessed of intelligence, and having the natural use of his limbs that will enable him to receive and impart Craft mysteries.

37. It is the internal qualifications of a man that recommend him to become a Mason.

38. Careful inquiry into the physical, intellectual and moral fitness of every candidate for the mysteries of Masonry is indispensable.

39. Advancement to the degrees of Fellow Craft or Master Mason is not to be made without examination as to the qualifications of the candidate.

40. Unanimous consent of the lodge, expressed by ballot, is essential before initiation, or admission to affiliation.

41. A Mason must be a good man and true, conforming to the laws of justice and virtue, called "the moral law."

42. Every Mason must be obedient to the laws of the country in which he lives.

43. No brother can recognize any one as a Mason until after strict trial or lawful examination.

44. A Mason is bound to use the utmost caution when in the presence of strangers or profanes, that no sign, token or word to which they may not be entitled shall be discovered by them.

45. Every Mason ought to belong to some regular lodge, attend its meetings, and share its burdens.

46. A brother is not to be admitted to lodge membership without certificate (of demit), due notice and inquiry.

47. Every Mason must patiently submit to the award of his brethren in lodge assembled, subject to appeal to Grand Lodge.

48. A Mason must be true to his fellow: instruct, admonish, defend and assist, but never traduce or supplant him.

49. A Mason shall not have unlawful knowledge of the wife, daughter, mother, sister or servant of his fellow.

50. A Mason should be diligent in business, and pay his just debts.

51. Every Mason must obey lodge summons.

52. The only penalties known to Masonry are fines, reprimand, suspension for a definite period and expulsion.

53. A Mason can not be disciplined without having the opportunity to be heard in his own defense, unless he absconds or can not be reached by notice.

54. Every (affiliated) Master Mason is entitled to burial with Masonic (ceremonies and) honors.

John W. Simons' Landmarks

1. A belief in the existence of a Supreme Being, and in the immortality of the soul.

2. That the moral law, which inculcates, among other things, charity and probity, industry and sobriety, is the rule and guide of every Mason.

3. Respect for, and obedience to, the civil law of the country, and the Masonic regulations of the jurisdiction where a Mason may reside.

4. That new-made Masons must be freeborn, of lawful age, and hale and sound at the time of making.

5. The modes of recognition, and, generally, the rites and ceremonies of the three degrees of Ancient Craft Masonry.

6. That no appeal can be taken to the Lodge, from the decision of the Master, or the Warden occupying the Chair in his absence.

7. That no one can be the Master of a Warranted Lodge until he has been installed and served one year as Warden.

8. That when a man becomes a Mason, he not only acquires membership in the particular lodge that admits him, but, in a general sense, he becomes one of the whole Masonic family; and hence he has a right to visit, Masonically, every regular

lodge, except when such visit is likely to disturb the harmony or interrupt the working of the lodge he proposes to visit.

9. The prerogative of the Grand Master to preside over every assembly of the Craft, within his jurisdiction, to make Masons at sight in a regular lodge, and to grant Dispensations for the formation of new lodges.

10. That no one can be made a Mason, save in a regular lodge, duly convened, after petition, and acceptance by unanimous ballot, except when made at sight by the Grand Master.

11. That the ballot for candidates is strictly and inviolably secret.

12. That a lodge cannot try its Master.

13. That every Mason is amenable to the laws and regulations of the jurisdiction in which he resides, even though he be a member of a particular lodge in some other jurisdiction.

14. The right of the Craft at large to be represented in Grand Lodge, and to instruct their representatives.

15. The general aim and form of the society, and handed down to us by the fathers, to be by use preserved inviolate, and transmitted to our successors forever.

Dr. Roscoe Pound's Landmarks

1. Belief in God.

2. Belief in the persistence of personality (immortality).

3. A "Book of the Law" as an indispensable part of the furniture of every Lodge.

4. The legend of the third degree.

5. Secrecy.

6. The symbolism of the operative art.

7. That a Mason must be a man, free born and of age.

PRAYER FOR FREEMASONS

As Christians, it is important that we educate the public (Masons and non-Masons alike) about the errors of Freemasonry and how Masonry is harmful to the Christian faith. But we must do more than educate. We must also win the spiritual battle for Christ. To that end, we must constantly pray for the conversion of Freemasons. We must ask the Lord to illumine these men with the light of his truth so that their minds and hearts will turn toward Jesus. Through our prayers and sacrifices, God will free these men from the grip of the Lodge and bring them into the joy of "the way, and the truth, and the life," Jesus Christ our Lord (Jn 14:6).

Here is a prayer that we can offer daily for the conversion of Freemasons:

> O Lord Jesus Christ, who showest forth Thine omnipotence most manifestly when Thou sparest and hast compassion, Thou who didst say, "Pray for those who persecute and calumniate thee," we implore the clemency of Thy Sacred Heart on behalf of souls made in the image of God, but most miserably deceived by the treacherous snares of Freemasonry, and going more and more astray in the way of

perdition. Let not the Church, Thy Spouse, any longer be oppressed by them, but appeased by the intercession of the Blessed Virgin, Thy Mother, and the prayers of the just, be mindful of Thy infinite mercy and, disregarding their perversity, cause these very men to return to Thee, that they may bring consolation to the Church by a most abundant penance, make reparation for their misdeeds, and secure for themselves a glorious eternity. Who livest and reignest, world without end. Amen.

BIBLIOGRAPHY OF SELECTED REFERENCES

In researching this book unmasking the religion of American Freemasonry, many Masonic documents from states throughout the country have been examined. These materials were compiled with the assistance of other former Masons who left the Lodge to follow Jesus Christ. Because most of these resources are distributed exclusively to Masons and thus available to the public only with great difficulty, they are not included in the bibliography. The following is a short list of resources that are available to the general public.

Acker, J. W. *Strange Altars: A Scriptural Appraisal of the Lodge*. St. Louis: Concordia, 1959.

Ankerberg, John and John Weldon. *The Secret Teachings of the Masonic Lodge*. Chicago: Moody Press, 1990.

Blackmer, Rolland C. *The Lodge and the Craft*. Richmond, Va.: Macoy, 1976.

Box, Hubert S. *The Nature of Freemasonry*. London: Augustine Press, 1952.

Canon Law Society of America. *New Commentary on the Code of Canon Law*. Edited by John P. Beal, James A. Cordien, and Thomas J. Green. Mahwah, N.J.: Paulist Press, 2000.

Catechism of the Catholic Church. Second Edition. Washington, D.C.: United States Catholic Conference, Inc., 1997.

Cerza, Alphonse. *"Let There Be Light": A Study in Anti-Masonry*. Silver Spring, Md.: Masonic Service Association, 1977.

Chase, George Wingate. *Digest of Masonic Law*. Third Edition. New York: Macoy and Sickles, 1864.

Chesterton, Gilbert K. *The Everlasting Man*. London: Hodder and Stoughton, 1925; reprint, San Francisco: Ignatius Press, 1974.

Claudy, Carl H. *Foreign Countries: A Gateway to the Interpretation and Development of Certain Symbols of Freemasonry*. Richmond, Va.: Macoy, 1971.

_____. *Introduction to Freemasonry*. Morristown, N.J.: Temple Publishers, 1931.

Codex Iuris Canonici (Code of Canon Law). Washington, D.C.: Canon Law Society of America, 1989.

Coil, Henry Wilson. *Coil's Masonic Encyclopedia*. New York: Macoy, 1961.

Fisher, Louis. *American Constitutional Law*. New York: McGraw-Hill, 1990.

Fisher, Paul. *Behind the Lodge Door*. Bowie, Md.: Shield Publishing Co., 1988; reprint, Rockford, Ill.: Tan Books and Publishers, 1994.

Friendly, Melvin. *Papers of Research Lodge of Oregon, No. 198 AF & AM*. Forest Grove, Ore.: Grand Lodge of Oregon A.F. & A.M., 1996.

Hall, Manly P. *An Encyclopedic Outline of Masonic, Hermetic, Qabbalistic and Rosicrucian Symbolical Philosophy*. Los Angeles: Philosophical Research Society, 1977.

_____. *The Lost Keys of Freemasonry; or The Secret of Hiram Abiff*. Richmond, Va.: Macoy, 1976.

Hannah, Walton. *Darkness Visible*. London: Augustine Press, 1952.

Harris, Jack. *Freemasonry: The Invisible Cult in Our Midst*. Towson, Md.: Jack Harris, 1983.

Haywood, H. L. *The Great Teachings of Masonry*. Richmond, Va.: Macoy, 1971.

Heirloom Masonic Bible. Master Reference Edition. Wichita, Kan.: DeVore & Sons, 1988.

Henderson, Kent. *Masonic World Guide — A Guide to Grand Lodges of the World for the Travelling Freemason.* London: Lewis Masonic, 1984; Richmond, Va.: Macoy, 1984.

Jackson, Robert H. *The Struggle for Judicial Supremacy.* New York: Alfred A. Knopf, 1941.

Kah, Gary H. *En Route to Global Occupation.* Lafayette, La.: Huntington House, 1991.

Knight, Stephen. *The Brotherhood: The Explosive Exposé of the Secret World of the Freemasons.* London: Granada/Panther, 1983.

Lacquement, Charles H. *The Pennsylvania Freemason.* Elizabethtown, Pa.: Masonic Homes, 1989.

Leaves from Georgia Masonry. Macon, Ga.: Educational and Historical Commission of the Grand Lodge of Georgia, 1947.

Little Masonic Library. Kingsport, Tenn.: Southern Publishers, Inc., 1946.

Mackey, Albert G. *Masonic Ritualist.* New York: Clark & Maynard, 1869.

_____. *Encyclopedia of Freemasonry.* Philadelphia: L. H. Everts, 1887.

_____. *Mackey's Revised Encyclopedia of Freemasonry.* Revised and enlarged by Robert I. Clegg. Richmond, Va.: Macoy, 1966.

Morgan, Captain William. *Freemasonry Exposed.* Batavia, N.Y.: William Morgan, 1827.

Newton, Joseph Fort. *The Builders: A Story and Study of Freemasonry.* Cedar Rapids, Iowa: The Torch Press, 1915; reprint, Richmond, Va.: Macoy, 1951.

_____. *The Religion of Masonry.* Richmond, Va.: Macoy, 1969.

Perkins, Lynn F. *The Meaning of Masonry: A Popular Guide to the Values of Ancient and Modern Freemasonry.* Lakemont, Ga.: CSA Press, 1960 (softcover edition, 1971).

Pike, Albert. *Morals and Dogma of the Ancient and Accepted Scottish Rite of Freemasonry.* Charleston, S.C.: Supreme Council of the

Thirty-third Degree for the Southern Jurisdiction of the United States, 1881.

Provost, James. *CLSA Advisory Opinions: 1984-1993*. Edited by Patrick Cogan. Washington, D.C.: Canon Law Society of America, 1995.

Roberts, Allen E. *The Craft and Its Symbols: Opening the Door to Masonic Symbolism*. Richmond, Va.: Macoy, 1974.

_____. *Key to Freemasonry's Growth*. Richmond, Va.: Macoy, 1969.

Ronayne, Edmond. *Ronayne's Handbook of Freemasonry*. Chicago: Edmond Ronayne, 1917; reprint, Whitefish, Mont.: Kessinger Publishing, 1998.

_____. *Master's Carpet; or Masonry and Baal Worship Identical*. Chicago: Edmond Ronayne, 1997; reprint, Whitefish, Mont.: Kessinger Publishing, 1998.

Sickles, Daniel. *"Ahimon Rezon" or "Freemason's Guide."* Columbia, S.C.: R. L. Bryan Company, 1965.

Simmons, George, and Robert Macoy. *Standard Masonic Monitor of the Degrees of Entered Apprentice, Fellow Craft, and Master Mason*. Richmond, Va.: Macoy, 1984.

Story, Joseph. *Commentaries on the Constitution of the United States*. Three volumes. Boston: Little, Brown and Co., 1865.

The Short Talk Bulletin. The Masonic Service Association of North America. Silver Spring, Md.: The Masonic Service Association of North America.

Wagner, Martin L. *Freemasonry: An Interpretation*. Dahlonega, Ga.: Crown Rights Book Company, 1912.

Webb, Thomas Smith. *The Freemason's Monitor*. Cincinnati: Pettibone Bros, 1797.

Whalen, William J. *Christianity and American Freemasonry*. Third Edition. San Francisco: Ignatius Press, 1987.

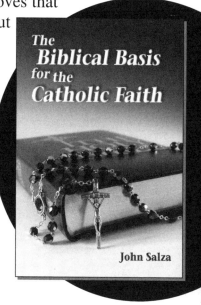